TO SURVIVE AND TO TELL THE STORY

CHAIM KURITSKY

Wasteland Press

www.wastelandpress.net
Shelbyville, KY USA

To Survive and To Tell the Story: A Memoir
by Chaim Kuritsky

First Printing – September 2013
ISBN: 978-1-60047-899-4
Translated from Hebrew by Ariella Gold.

Front cover painting of the Vilna Ghetto by Chaim Kuritsky.
Reproduction by Ayala Don

Printed in the U.S.A.

0   1   2   3   4   5   6   7   8   9

FOREWORD

Chaim Kuritsky was twenty years old on June 22, 1941, when, as
part of Operation Barbarossa, the Nazi German forces invaded
Soviet Lithuania and advanced on the city of Utian where Chaim
was born and where his forefathers had lived for some two
hundred years. The local Jewish community was considered to be
one of the oldest in Lithuania and, between the two world wars,
numbered approximately three thousand residents, about half of
the total population. Hence, the city had two Jewish mayors during
this period. In addition to its various religious, educational, and
welfare institutions and numerous other Jewish organizations, the
city was known for its cultural and political activities affiliated with
the Left.

Since Utian is located at the northeastern edge of Lithuania,
near the Latvian and Belarusan border, it took some time before
the German forces entered the city. These circumstances enabled
the Jewish population to flee eastward by car or by foot toward
Russia. The Jewish flight was motivated by fear of what awaited
them in Utian, both at the hands of the German soldiers and at the
hands of their Lithuanian neighbors, who did not conceal their
cruel intentions. Among those who managed to escape were
Chaim's sisters, Chaya and Sarah, who found refuge in the Soviet

Union until after the war. In contrast, Chaim, who refused to abandon his mother, stayed with her and accompanied her on foot on a lengthy, grueling trek eastward. Following numerous harrowing ordeals, they finally reached Dvinsk (Daugavpils) in Latvia, where they were brutally arrested by German soldiers, who separated them. While Chaim was imprisoned in the local jail, his mother was brought to the ghetto and sent to work in a military kitchen.

About a month later, when Chaim managed to miraculously escape execution, he was able to see his mother a couple of times. However, in August 1941, he lost her forever. Like tens of thousands of other single women, she was executed during one of the aktions in the Dvinsk ghetto. Undoubtedly, the loss of his gentle mother, whom he greatly adored, left him with a critical gaping wound for many years. It is not a coincidence that approximately one-third of the following book is dedicated to this traumatic chapter, which occurred over a relatively short period of time: only about two months.

Riveting tales of devotion and love—especially between those from the same town or region—took place even in the Nazi hell. The tales, which Chaim recorded "in real time" over the course of four years, on the lost pages of his journal, are told modestly and without embellishment. Throughout that period, Chaim waged a daily war of survival in the ghetto and in the various concentration camps until he was liberated on May 5, 1945, in a remote German village called Mantz.

Like many survivors, he returned to his country of origin. He married, had children, and remained in Lithuania for a quarter of a century before making *aliyah* (moving to Israel) in 1971. In Israel, Chaim settled in Kfar Saba and made an honest living. During his free time, he was involved in the arts and public activities, particularly those concerning Utian Jewry. For instance, he was an active member of the Committee for the Publication of a Memorial Volume for Utian and Its Environs. This book was published in Tel Aviv in 5739 (1979) under the title, *Yizkor Buch: Utian Un Umgegant* (*Memorial Book: Utian and Its Environs*) and contained some three hundred pages, most of them in Yiddish. The volume included some of Chaim Kuritsky's writings:

1. An article about his experiences in Utian during the war's outbreak.
2. A poem called "Underer Treist" ("Our Consolation"). In this poem, he expresses his happiness upon moving to Israel (Zion), which envelops him in a mother's gentle embrace. Clearly this imagery alludes to his own mother, whose image is still with him here. Indeed, he underwent a long period of torment before he could write about his experiences during the Holocaust in general, and his pain at losing her in particular. However, he was greatly encouraged by his family: his late wife, his three daughters, and his eight grandchildren. The latter served as a strong motivation for him to overcome the psychological difficulty of returning to that agonizing topic and to publish his words in Hebrew for his daughters, his grandchildren, and their descendants.

Professor Dov Levin
The Institute for Contemporary Judaism
Hebrew University
10 Cheshvan 5761, Jerusalem

CONTENTS

INTRODUCTION

As the Nazis—may their names be obliterated—tried to ensure that there would be no living witnesses to their barbaric crimes, I became increasingly determined to elude their bloodstained talons and document their sins against my people.

To this end, I gathered information in real time on any scrap of paper that I happened to find. Due to the circumstances, I was frequently forced to destroy my writing and then rewrite it later.

Immediately following my liberation from the inferno and my conscription into the Red Army, I used my free time to recreate everything I had endured based on the memories that were still fresh in my mind. I wrote in Yiddish, my mother tongue. Eventually, I produced a sort of journal, which I then gave to my good friend from Dvinsk, Avraham Kanolik, who had been released from the army and returned to his hometown. In late 1946, when I was demobilized as well, I traveled to Dvinsk to collect my journal from him.

When I made aliyah (moved to Israel) with my family in July 1971, I took my journal with me and hoped to present it to Yad Vashem. My wife Luba, of blessed memory, outsmarted the Russian border guards, and, to our great joy, her mission was a success. I gave a copy of my journal to Yad Vashem.

In 1992 at the encouragement of my friend, Professor Dov Levin, I translated part of my journal into Hebrew and received an award from the Association of Latvian Jews in Israel. The translation was added to the association's archives in Kibbutz Shefayim. In due course, I translated the rest of the material into Hebrew.

Many other details from my difficult life during the Holocaust remained in my memory, and I felt that it was important that they be documented.

I wish to thank my second wife, Chaya Kaplan—may she be distinguished by a long life—who encouraged me to continue to record my memoirs.

Thank you also to Professor Dov Levin, who wrote the foreword to my book, and to my friend, the noted artist, Moshe Rosenthalis, who devoted a number of his drawings to my book's content.

And finally, thank you to my grandson, Daniel Kremer, whose dedicated efforts led to my book's publication.

I hope that this work will serve as a significant contribution to the field of Holocaust research for our nation's future generation and for anyone who is interested in this painful subject.

Chaim Kuritsky
Holon, Israel
1 Kislev 5761

MY BACKGROUND

I was born on January 8, 1921 (28 Tevet 5681) in Utian, a district capital in northeastern Lithuania. The majority of the city's residents were Jewish.

On my mother's side, I can list the names of the four generations who preceded me and lived in Utian: My mother, Liba Raizel, was born in 1898 to her father, Yosef Yaakov Sharfshtein, and her mother, Chaya nee Eisen. My mother's parents were born in the early 1870s. My grandfather Yosef Yaakov Sharfshtein's parents were Moshe and Sarah Sharfshtein. Moshe Sharfshtein's parents, Ephraim and Fruma Sharfshtein, were born in the early nineteenth century in Utian.

My father, Tzvi Hirsh Kuritsky, was born in the town of Vidzh in eastern Poland in 1895. He was the fourth son of Baruch and Shayna. Their eldest son was Yerachmiel, followed by Rafael and Avraham.

My parents got married in Utian in the fall of 1919, and my father became a successful leather merchant. His business flourished, and he even built two imposing stone buildings in the center of town.

In February 1922, my brother Moshe was born, and my sister Chaya was born in September 1923.

Lithuania was struck by a severe economic crisis in 1925, and my father's business was hit hard. Unable to recover from his financial difficulties, he had no choice but to sell his assets, and we were forced to move to a rented apartment in late 1925.

In March 1926, my younger sister Sarah was born. When she was a mere six weeks old, my father left for South Africa and continued on from there to Australia. During the next two years, he regularly sent us letters and money to support us, but then all communication stopped. Thanks to my mother's hard work and the help of her relatives in the United States, Brazil, and Palestine, we managed somehow to eke out a living.

Moshe, Chaya, and I completed seven years at the school and the progymnasium. Hebrew was the primary language of instruction, and we also studied Lithuanian, German, and Latin. Our little sister Sarah attended the Tarbut School and then the Lithuanian gymnasium.

After leaving school, my brother Moshe and I worked hard as painters, and Chaya worked as a secretary in a governmental office in our town in order to support the family. During the winters, all three of us tutored students who needed help with their schoolwork, and we even delivered newspapers.

On June 6, 1940, my brother Moshe died of tuberculosis at the Remainiai Sanatorium near Kovno. For the next year, from June 15 when the Soviets entered Lithuania until war broke out between Germany and Soviet Russia, I continued to work as a painter. In the evenings, I continued my studies at the city's Lithuanian gymnasium, together with my sister Chaya. Before the Soviets arrived in Lithuania, I was active in the local HaShomer HaTzair chapter, and during the Soviet period, I got involved in the Komsomol, the Soviet youth movement.

In 1934 we received a letter from my father, expressing deep remorse over his prolonged silence. He defended himself by explaining that he did not have the means to help us, and he could not bear to send us empty letters. Apparently, his financial situation did not improve because we did not hear from him again until 1939. We then received another letter in which he repeated his request for forgiveness. He also asked that we find a way to join him in Australia, claiming that then everything would be fine.

However, by that time, Poland was at war with Germany, and it became impossible for us to leave Lithuania. To this day, my father's fate remains unknown.

CHAPTER ONE:

The Beginning of the War and Leaving Utian

On Sunday morning, June 22, 1941, I woke up a bit later than usual because it was the day of rest.

After a relaxed breakfast with my family—my mother, Liba Raizel, and my sisters, Chaya, nearly seventeen, and Sarah, fifteen—I headed out with a friend from the town of Maliat, who happened to be staying with us, to a Lithuanian school, which was located not too far from the center of town.

It was already 9:00 a.m. when we arrived at a certain spot next to the school, the exact time and place where we, the future soldiers of the Red Army, were to undergo pre-military training.

We waited about fifteen minutes for our army trainer, but he never showed up, so we decided to train on our own at a nearby soccer field. Within a few minutes, we reached the soccer field where we were in for a surprise. Pietrus Kotka, chairman of Utian's Communist party branch, suddenly arrived and told us that we must go home because the field was going to be used for other purposes that day.

We all set off in different directions without understanding the reason behind the sudden change in plans. My friend went to our house, and I walked to the post office on the side of the road, which divided our city in half. I subscribed to the Yiddish monthly *Shtralen* (Sunrays) for July.

From there, I returned to the area near the soccer field, to the fire station, to collect money for newspapers they had recently received from me. As I entered the fire station office, I noticed that the firemen were listening to the news in German on a hand-operated radio. Their faces were extremely strained. I paid close attention to the things being said in a furious voice about the Jews, the Bolsheviks, and so on. I sensed that something had suddenly and unexpectedly happened in the world and that this was not the time to approach them about settling debts. Instead it would be best if I went home to be with my family.

As soon as I stepped outside, I met an acquaintance who informed me that at 4:00 a.m. that day, war had suddenly broken out between Germany and the Soviet Union.

Lately, we felt that the tension between the two countries had increased, but nevertheless the news hit me like a thunderbolt on a clear day. Since I was near the Komsomol's central offices, I decided to step inside and ascertain what we, the youth, were supposed to do under the new circumstances.

Together with another friend, Shabtai Katzav, I was assigned a mission: to go from house to house along the main street and instruct the residents about what they were supposed to do, how to conduct themselves during wartime due to the blackout, how to find shelter in case of a German aerial attack, what was permitted, what was forbidden, and so on.

We started out at the city's southern end near the train station at around 11:00 a.m., and by the time we were finished, it was already 2:00 p.m. I took leave of my friend and arrived home, tired, anxious, and hungry. My family had been waiting impatiently for my return. They were aware of the abrupt change in the situation, but their faces did not yet show any signs of panic or fear. After eating lunch, I went to listen to a neighbor's radio to gather any additional news. Suddenly, I heard Radio Moscow playing reassuring marches and Molotov's speech. I was slightly encouraged. Later that afternoon, I met up with some friends to discuss the day's events. We all agreed that the war would last no more than half a year. I returned home, nervous about what was going on in the world, but I did not share my concerns with my family. After supper, we all went to sleep much earlier than usual.

Monday, June 23

At 7:00 a.m., I was awakened by my mother's distraught voice, "How were you able to sleep so soundly? The girls and I spent a sleepless night because of the deafening roar of the German airplanes, which terrorized the city's residents and fired over the rooftops."

After listening to what she said, I immediately threw on my clothes, grabbed a bite for breakfast, and went out to see if I could pick up any news from our neighbors and acquaintances. According to the rumors, which had been circulating among the city's residents, the Germans had captured a number of Lithuanian towns in the southern part of the country, and their army was advancing towards Kovno!

Several of my friends and I went to the bus station and saw that the street was packed with refugees in cars, in wagons, and on foot. They were coming from Kovno, Yanova, and Ukmerga. Among them, I observed buses filled with the soldiers' families, militias, state employees, and regular civilians who had managed to climb aboard. On one of the buses, I noticed a relative, Masha Eisen, whose husband, Chaim, was my mother's cousin and a high-ranking official in the Soviet government in Lithuania. She asked me to inform our relatives as soon as possible that the situation was critical and extremely dangerous and that we should try to leave town and head to the Soviet border!

A few minutes later, as I was trying to get home quickly to tell my family what I had heard, a siren went off, and I ran to the municipal park on the main street in order to find a place to hide. I had never before been that frightened in my life. After the initial scare, when everything had calmed down and the German bombers were gone, I sped home, but to my dismay, my family was not there. The front door was bolted with a padlock. I immediately ran off to search for them and finally found them in a neighbor's basement. There was enough room in the basement for several families who lived nearby.

The basement and the house belonged to a woman named Mina Weinerman, and her son, Yitzchak, was a good friend of mine. I stepped into their kitchen, ate something, and told my mother that my older sister Chaya, our cousin Zelda, and I were going to the community center to find out what was going on. (The two girls belonged to the Komsomol youth movement, but I was not a member.) It was there that I learned that Kovno had been captured by the German Army! Unable to wrap my mind around the news, I went over to a neighbor who had a radio to confirm the truth of what we had heard. It occurred to me that if the Germans were in Kovno less than a day after the war had begun, Lithuanian Jewry was in dire straits. My short visit to the house meant that I had lost the chance to leave our town by car.

Reshel, my grandfather's sister who lived next door to us, took advantage of the opportunity and, together with her pregnant daughter Fruma, her two daughters and son, left Utian in a truck. My mother and my two sisters could have joined them, but they did not want to leave me behind.

Aunt Reshel's two sons, Yitzchak and Ephraim, were still at home, and they intended to depart early the next morning toward the Russian border.

That evening, we gloomily grabbed a few essential items from our home, and the four of us went to the community center to ask my father's cousin Berman Avraham, a senior party official, to help us reach the Russian border. He promised that he would try to assist us the next morning.

That same Monday afternoon, after we had lost our chance of getting a ride to the Soviet border, I went with Rafael Feller, a friend who lived on our street, to Utian's military commander. Our question was what to do under the new circumstances, given that we were soon to become soldiers of the Red Army. He replied laconically, "Do whatever you want." Thus, we had no choice but to spend the night with our cousins and then leave the city with them first thing in the morning. On the way to their house, we stopped off at home in order to find something to eat before going to bed.

Tuesday, June 24

We were unable to close our eyes during that short summer night because the enemy's planes flew overhead, and every so often, we even heard the reverberations of nearby explosions. In addition, the painful recognition that the next morning we were to become refugees prevented us from getting any sleep. At dawn, we got out of bed, ate whatever food was left from the day before, took the packages that we had been carrying from yesterday afternoon, and set out together with our cousins.

When we passed our house, we unlocked the door, went inside, and grabbed a few valuables that Mother had kept throughout the years in case of emergency. We left our family's picture albums behind, but we took the new identity cards, which Chaya, our mother, and I had recently acquired. Our mother had three *chervonets* (one chervonets equaled ten rubles), and she gave one to each of the children in case we would be separated.

For food, she took some herring and half a loaf of bread, and we all carried our coats, lest we would be forced to sleep under the stars. On the way out, we locked the door with a padlock, and with a faint glimmer of hope that perhaps we would be back, we were on our way.

As we headed toward the main road that divided our town into two parts, we knew that we had a long journey ahead of us to the Soviet border. We had never hiked dozens of kilometers at a time. My sisters and I, I mused, would manage, but for our mother, who had long suffered from aches and pains in her legs, the challenge would be too great. I told myself that whatever happened, I would not abandon my mother.

We passed through the city's deserted streets, which were still engulfed in the nighttime fog. Our cousins walked with us at the same pace, but when we reached the main road, they left us.

An emotional scene is still burned in my memory: One of our neighbors, a porter by trade, was carrying one child on his shoulders and holding another one by the hand. Suddenly, he stopped on the side of the main road and cried out, "Where should we go now?!"

As we traveled northward on the road, we noticed groups of families, spread out in every direction. Some sought shelter with farmers in the villages, others stopped off at the adjacent towns, and still others continued on toward the Soviet border, like us. Half a kilometer down the road, we noticed our relative, Avraham Berman, driving by. His wife, who was nearing the end of her pregnancy, sat beside him. He saw our eyes pleading with him for help, but he motioned in a way that said, 'What can I do? My car is full...'

All of a sudden, a siren blared, and all the refugees who were fleeing northward scattered to the sides of the road, seeking shelter. The four of us also turned right off the road. However, at that very moment, a vehicle nearly filled with the city's firefighters drove by, and my sister Sarah joined them.

The three of us continued to trudge northward. At one point, when we were already about two kilometers out of the city, we heard a massive explosion coming from the city. When we turned around and saw fire and smoke billowing from the center of town, we sensed that we had left the city of our birth just in time.

A number of fellow Utian refugees overtook us and reported that the main street, Kovno Street, had been particularly hard hit by the explosions. The wooden houses were in flames, and apparently, there were many casualties.

By the time we arrived in the town of Radeikiai, located some ten kilometers north of Utian, we had started to feel the exhaustion and the strain. We rested for a bit and then continued onward. The stream of refugees increased. Most of them were on foot, but here and there, the refugees were interspersed with vehicles. One such vehicle proved to be a nearly empty bus, which was carrying Communist party members from Kovno to the Russian border. The bus came to a brief stop, and we thought that we would be allowed to board. However, we were distressed to discover that they were taking only members of the Komsomol or the party. My sister, Chaya, who worked as a clerk at the party's offices and was carrying a document to that effect, was permitted to join the

13

passengers. But my mother and I, who could not prove that we were members of the Communist party, remained outside.

Yitzchak Weinerman, our town's Communist party treasurer, who was good friends with my sister and me, was also on the bus. He had taken all the money in the account with him in order to transfer it to Russia. However, he, too, was unable to get us on the bus. We begged the people in charge to let us board, but to our dismay, they were indifferent to our pleas. Thus we lost our final chance to be evacuated by car. We consoled ourselves with the knowledge that at least Chaya and Sarah had found rides and that there was a good chance that they could cross the Russian border before being overtaken by the Germans.

I felt very bad for my poor mother and her aching feet. She was forced to walk many kilometers in the summer heat toward the unknown future. Yet, on the other hand, I believed that this was the only option we had left.

We had traveled about thirty kilometers by foot in the direction of Zarasai, which was located approximately fifty kilometers from our city. On the way, we met young Jews from the towns of Antaliept, Dusiat, Maliat, and Saluk, and they told us that the Lithuanian nationalists were cruelly murdering the local Jews. The panicked and frightened Jews were attempting to flee from the awful fate which awaited them in their hometowns. When we heard these reports, we became even more determined to escape the menacing evil.

The German bombers intermittently dropped bombs on the road, which was packed with the refugees' vehicles and the retreating Red Army's tanks. But most of the traffic were pedestrians and, of course, the Jews who feared for their lives.

A newly married couple from Utian—Abba and Bluma Katz, who worked as hairdressers—joined us, and together, we decided to enter a Lithuanian family's home and grab a bite.

The woman pretended to take pity on us, our fate, and our new refugee status and quietly invited us into one of the rooms, where we would be able to eat some of our food. We then noticed that her husband had suddenly disappeared. A quick look out the window revealed that he was sharpening a number of long knives, and his objective was obvious. We immediately left their house and continued on our way.

When we were some ten kilometers from Zarasai, we met our cousin, Tzvi Sharfshtein, who was walking with some other young guys his age. He told us that his two sisters and their families had managed to get a ride to the northeast and that the Jews were fleeing Nazi-occupied Kovno in every direction. In addition, he reported that the nationalist Lithuanians were attacking the fleeing Jews and that it was a miracle that they had escaped. We said goodbye to Tzvi and his friends, who still had the ability to reach the Russian border.

My mother and I entered the forest on the right side of the road in order to rest our weary bones. When darkness fell, we found shelter in an abandoned school, which was already packed with Jewish refugees. We lay down on the wooden floor, and because we were so tired, we fell asleep immediately.

Wednesday, June 25

We arose at dawn. A Russian family who lived nearby gave us half a loaf of black bread and some water. The entire group of Jewish refugees, who happened to gather in the abandoned school, walked toward Zarasai, that lovely city, which burned before our eyes.

The steady stream of retreating Russian tanks grew heavier. We walked between them and proved to be easy targets for the German bombers. Lithuanian nationalist snipers shot at us from a church tower. Miraculously, we escaped this danger even though they commanded a large swath of the city from above. The dead lay on the street, and no one bothered to move them.

At the city's northern edge, Soviet sentinels inspected us and permitted us to advance toward the Latvian border, which was located some three kilometers ahead. We crossed the border without any trouble because no one was guarding it.

Once we were on Latvian soil, we met up with a fairly large group of Jewish refugees from Kovno. We walked into a Latvian farmer's house, and after we paid him, he gave us some food, which we ate with great relish. We rested a bit and then started walking toward the city of Dvinsk (i.e. Daugavpils in Latvian), which was located about twenty-five kilometers from Zarasai.

For us, the refugees walking between the numerous tanks and vehicles, which served as constant targets for the shelling, became a real nightmare. Every so often, we stretched out on the sides of the road in fright until the bombers had gone by.

During one such shelling in the evening, when many bombers circled overhead and shot in every direction, my mother and I exchanged coverings a few times, and I lost my winter coat, which held my papers—my new identity card and the document labeling me as a future soldier of the Red Army.

After nightfall, we picked up our pace and continued toward Dvinsk in order to reach the train station as early as possible. Our hope was that we would meet Chaya and Sarah there, and then together, we could all escape to the East. The German aerial attacks ceased during the night. Five members of a Jewish family from Zarasai, named Shaltoffer, joined us. The father was a tailor by profession. Their two sons, who were about my age, and a younger daughter accompanied him and his wife. Among other things, they brought material for suits. Since it was hard for them to carry the fabric, and I was cold at night without my coat, I asked them to give me some cloth to put under my shirt. In this way, I managed to withstand the cold nighttime air.

After walking all night without rest, including several shortcuts through fields and marshes, we arrived at the outskirts of Dvinsk early in the morning. We passed Griva, a suburb of Dvinsk, and when we reached the iron bridge spanning the Dvina River, German airplanes suddenly appeared and began firing at the refugees crossing into the city. Since we were already on the bridge, we took a chance and managed to reach the other side without being hit.

As we hurried down several of the city's main streets on our way to the train station, we saw local Jewish residents coming out of their houses and giving us looks, which spoke of their identification with our shared fate. We crossed Riga Street and arrived at the train station, which was crowded with refugees. In the station, we met someone from our town who told us that Chaya and Sarah had left the day before by train to Russia, together with Kalman Goldfein's family. Our feelings were mixed. On one hand, we were sorry that fate had separated us and that we had no idea when we would meet again. But on the other hand, we were glad that at least they had managed to escape eastward. Shortly thereafter, we noticed that a certain Jew was compiling a list of Jewish refugees who wished to be evacuated to the East. Needless to say, we signed up.

Before we had a chance to catch our breath after everything we had endured, we heard a siren indicating that the German bombers had returned. We briefly descended into the bomb shelter, and when we came out, we heard the train's whistle as it left the station. Thus, we missed yet another opportunity to escape the mortal danger, which was breathing down our necks.

We exited the waiting room and walked over to the platforms where a Soviet border guard stopped me for an inspection because he thought I looked suspicious. He was concerned by my body's "bloated" appearance, which was caused by the fabric I had wrapped around myself. I removed the extra "baggage" and ran with my mother to a different train, which was standing on the platform and packed with refugees. They tried to storm the train, which was traveling to Riga, the Latvian capital.

Despondent, my mother did not want to board the train, but I insisted that we not give up on our last chance to escape. Using all my strength, I lifted her on to the car, and with the help of the people who were being pushed toward the car from behind us, we were both swept on board.

My mother sat down on one of the benches in the corner, and I climbed on to the bunk above her. Within a short time, after the train had begun to move westward, I fell asleep due to a combination of the heat, the crowded conditions, and exhaustion.

The train arrived at the first station on its way to the North— Mezciems, also known as Pogulyanka, an enormous area covered with pine trees. In early summer, the place would fill up with vacationers of every stripe, especially the Jews of Dvinsk.

Suddenly, a huge explosion rocked the car, and I found myself on top of those sitting on the benches below. No one knew what had caused the explosion, but it was clear that something had forced the train to a standstill. We waited for some time for the train to start moving again, but when the heat and the strain became unbearable, someone volunteered to go outside and find out why the train was sitting still so long. The sixteen-year-old volunteer was Micha Kovlentz from the city of Zarasai.

When he returned, he told us, with a panic-stricken face, that the area around our train was teeming with armed soldiers in green uniforms, that some of them were approaching, and that the train's engineer had fled. When he finished speaking, the frightened Jews began destroying any Russian currency that they had, lest the Germans seize their valuables and documents.

Within a few minutes, German paratroopers had opened the railway car doors and shouted in German, "All Jews? Outside! At once!"

We stepped out of the car with downcast eyes as if we had been sentenced to death. The German soldiers ordered us into the nearby thicket and had us kneel down in groups of three. Meanwhile, they positioned themselves in front of us and cocked their automatic weapons. My mother and I kissed each other as we prepared to leave this world.

Then, all of the sudden, the soldiers' commander approached and told them to let us go! They allowed us to go back into the car in order to collect any food or personal items we had left behind and then start walking toward Riga.

We divided all the food we found in the car among us and then went outside to rest from the tension we had just experienced. The hand of fate had instantaneously transformed us into one big family.

It was now obvious that our fate was sealed. We had nowhere to run. The dreaded German Army had caught up with us.

As evening approached, we saw that Dvinsk was in flames as a result of the Germans' relentless shelling. All around us, the Red Army battled the Germans; the fighting had apparently reached the outskirts of Dvinsk. The bombing reverberated through the air, but as long as the battles continued, we still hoped that perhaps the German Army would soon be routed and retreat. Perhaps?

My mother summed up her appraisal of the situation, "My son, look how much suffering this war has caused, and it's only the beginning. I'm not sure that we're going to get through this."

The entire group moved and scattered to the left of the railway and the bridge where we had remained until nightfall. My mother and I found a deep pit where we decided to spend the night. Although the fighting continued all around us, we were so tired that we both slept through the night.

Friday, June 27

When we woke up early the next morning, everything was quiet. There were no explosions, no artillery shelling, and no firing from automatic weapons. It was as if the war had ended. But unfortunately, the quiet did not mean that the situation had improved. Rather, it was a sign that the Germans had captured the city of Dvinsk from the retreating Red Army. Nevertheless, we wanted to go to Riga.

After walking two kilometers along the railroad tracks, we came to a Latvian's house. We knocked on the door and asked for some bread and a cup of milk. The previous day's food was gone, and we were hungry and thirsty. However, the Latvian refused to give us any food and asked that we leave before the Germans catch him harboring Jews. He gave us a bit of water and then demanded that we go quickly.

We walked about another kilometer northward, and then we noticed a forest off to the left of the railroad tracks. Since we did not anticipate any danger there and we needed a short rest, we decided to remain in the woods until after nightfall. Luckily, local farmers brought us enough bread and milk for everyone.

Most of the refugees in our group were from Kovno and Yanova. We introduced ourselves and exchanged amusing stories from our recent past to take our minds off our current circumstance. But it did not help.

We kept hoping that we would hear the sounds of nearby cannons because that would indicate that all was not lost. But it did not happen.

After darkness fell, we were afraid of staying in the forest. Therefore, one of our fellow refugees, who had once served in the Lithuanian Army, bravely volunteered to go find a sympathetic local who would be willing to hide us. Remarkably, an older Latvian farmer, his wife, and their young daughter agreed to take us in. There were about ten people in our group.

With a broad smile, the daughter readily went off to prepare food and drink for us. Her only request was that in these troubled times, when no could trust anyone else, we not show our faces outside their home. They were even wary of their own neighbors.

Following an ample meal, the kind farmer led us into his barn where we would be able to spend the night. The barn was filled with straw, and thus, for the first time since leaving home, we slept comfortably and deeply. We slept in our clothes, but that did not bother us.

Saturday, June 28

When we awoke that morning, our wonderful hosts brought us potatoes, which my mother and the other women peeled for cooking. Throughout the day, the farmer and his family supplied us with food and drink, including hot soup. We did not know how to thank these incredible people, who demonstrated such amazing humanity in a time of crisis. Since none of us knew any Latvian, we spoke to our hosts in Russian. They became very dear to us, and we were greatly encouraged by their words, in spite of the tense quiet and our uncertain future. Together, we tried to find some sort of solution—even a temporary one—to our predicament. Some of our group suggested that if the German Army had not yet captured Dvinsk, we should not sit and wait for a miracle. Instead, we should try to get to Riga. But how were we to know?!

Sadly, our group included a number of people who had lost their loved ones while fleeing from their hometowns. These wretched individuals resembled hurt and hounded animals, and they dejectedly repeated the names of their missing relatives over and over again.

We realized that that day would have to be the only day of our stay in the friendly farmer's house. The next day, we would have to move on.

Late that evening, we once again went to sleep in the barn.

CHAPTER TWO:

The Dvinsk Prison

Sunday, June 29, 1941

That summer morning, our entire group of Jewish refugees from Lithuania, including my mother and me, woke up early. As on the previous day, the goodhearted Latvian farmer, who, with his wife and young daughter, had provided us shelter when we were fleeing the German Army, gave us plenty of food for breakfast.

After we had finished eating, the farmer told us that their lives were in danger. The Germans, who had captured the entire area including Dvinsk, had posted notices informing the population that anyone caught harboring Jews would be sentenced to death. Therefore, to his sorrow, they would no longer be able to hide us. In addition, the notices declared that every Jewish man, between the ages of sixteen and twenty in Dvinsk must assemble at the city's market square at noon on Sunday, June 29. Those who disobeyed the orders would be put to death!

We realized that we had no choice but to say a thankful goodbye to our wonderful hosts and to head to the market square.

Before we left, the farmer and his family gave us as much food as they could, including bread, hardboiled eggs, and more.

On the way, we were stopped by German soldiers on motorcycles. When they saw that we were Jewish, they ordered us to hurry to the assembly point because, they said, the German Army needed Jews as a labor force.

Several minutes before noon, we arrived at the city's market square and saw a huge crowd of Jews. The square was packed with men, women, babies, and even the elderly. Their faces spoke of their sense of despair and helplessness. Everyone roamed around, looking for their family members and trying to stay together. At that moment, our hearts pounded in agony and fear. We were rendered speechless.

My mother and I noticed a woman and her three small children in the crowd. They had been our next-door neighbors for several years. Her name was Sorel, and she told us that early that morning, her husband Yosef Katz (a shoemaker by trade) had been forcibly removed from his sister's house. (The sister had been living in Dvinsk for the past few years.) According to the Germans, he was being sent to forced labor, together with other Jewish men.

Meanwhile, our entire group, which had been sheltered by the Latvian farmer and his family, joined the crowd. Everyone was filled with trepidation about what the next day would bring. We all tried to guess what the Germans were planning to do to us. It was a very hot day, and the sun's rays beat down on us. Fatigue and exhaustion were rampant. I had a short discussion with my mother, and we agreed that if the Germans sent me to forced labor, we would meet afterward at a certain spot in that square.

My mother still had a good impression of the German Army from their treatment of Utian Jewry during World War I. She would often tell us children about the friendships that her family had developed with the German soldiers. In fact, her father, Yosef Yaakov Sharfshtein, had owned a bakery, which provided bread for the German Army. Thus she hoped that the Germans would treat the Jews fairly and demonstrate their humanity now, although after eight years of the Nazi regime's venomous and hostile propaganda, their attitudes toward us had probably changed for the worse.

Suddenly, above our heads, we heard the strident shouts of husky-throated German soldiers. Dressed in green uniforms with iron plates, which read *GOTT IST MIT UNS* (GOD IS WITH US), these soldiers were dragging a large group of Jews who had been forcibly removed from their places of residence. As they marched loudly, the Germans yelled at the top of their voices and ordered all the Jews who had come by themselves to the square to join those who had been brought there.

In order to avoid the Nazi savages' strikes and blows and recognizing that I had no other choice, I decided to say goodbye to my mother and obey the Germans' command. My mother gave me a small piece of black bread with a boiled egg, which was all that we had received from the Latvian farmer and his family. Without shedding any tears, my mother and I kissed each other heartily, and I soon joined the large group of Jews.

For the next hour or so, which seemed like an eternity to us, the Germans mercilessly forced us to run through Dvinsk's main streets, which were now fenced off with barbed wire. Our feet stumbled and we fell. We resembled a browbeaten flock of sheep. My mother's final sorrowful and grief-stricken expression, which spoke of hopelessness in the face of the tragic, unknown future, rose before my eyes.

After running through several of the city's boroughs, we were crammed like cattle into the large prison courtyard, which extended along the eastern side of the road connecting Leningrad (St. Petersburg) with Warsaw.

Before we had a chance to unwind from the emotional strain and physical fatigue, we suddenly noticed a large group of Germans standing on the adjacent, overhead road. They were armed with machine guns and automatic weapons. A moment later, a tall German officer stood before us, and his mouth spewed ugly and vituperative obscenities about our nation. As he cursed us, he declared that we had only three minutes left to say our final prayers before every one of us would be shot.

Our Jewish brothers' heartrending cries and moans filled the air. It seemed to us that those three minutes would last forever. Meanwhile, the German soldiers began firing their weapons in the air to frighten us even more and to crush our spirits even further. After those few minutes had passed, the cruel officer turned to us again and said, "If a quorum of ten Jews steps forward and agrees to be shot, the remaining men will be allowed to live."

Suddenly, a tall, slender Jew whose face was covered by a yellowish beard (we later learned that he was the *Dayan*, the rabbinical judge, of Dvinsk) raised his hands. And immediately, many other Jews followed his lead and raised their hands as well. They were all willing to be killed to save their Jewish brothers.

"I see, then, that you are compatriots who are willing to sacrifice your lives for each other," the same officer bellowed. "And therefore, you'll all be kept alive for now. But you must thank and praise the Fuhrer, and together you must loudly cheer '*Heil Hitler*' and '*Deutschland, Deutschland über alles.*'"

An inarticulate murmur filled the air. The officer continued, "You will work for us. You are a herd of swine, and in order for you to become quick and industrious laborers, you will be required to do exercises and calisthenics."

Young Germans, wearing yellow uniforms with swastikas on their arms, suddenly entered the prison courtyard and started to "instruct" the elderly and weakest men, while heaping curses and invectives, punching and slapping them. Whoever did the training exercises earned the "privilege" of running into the three-storied prison building. Within about two hours, every room and jail cell was full.

With murder in their eyes, they roughly shoved us into those cells. The crowding was unbearable. It was impossible to sit down. We were forced to lie on top of one another. There was no food, no drink, and no way for us to relieve ourselves. It was excruciating torture, neither life nor death.

The windows were sealed shut with an iron grille, which was covered with an inverted wooden pyramid. Through it, we could glimpse a bit of the sky, but there was no way to see what was happening on the ground. Our thirst and the stifling lack of air were oppressive, but we were especially tormented by our thoughts: What was to become of us? What diabolical schemes were the barbaric Germans plotting against us?

Such was our first introduction to the Germans, Hitler's messengers who sought to annihilate us, on that Sunday, which is engraved in my memory forever.

Monday, June 30

The night before, I could not fall asleep. Slumber eluded me, and an atmosphere of terror pervaded the cell. Finally, just before dawn, I slept briefly. Early that morning, I thought about our terrible predicament and the staggering calamity, which had befallen us. We all realized that it was only because we were Jewish that we had ended up in this agonizing situation.

I told myself that there was nothing to do. We must simply gnash our teeth and keep quiet. We must not utter a single word. Crying was futile, and protesting would not help. We must accept everything in silence.

Throughout the day, they starved us and did not even offer us any water to drink. In the evening, the iron door of our cell opened, and German and Latvian guards allowed us to walk in groups to the latrine at the end of the long hallway. In the latrine, the guards let us swallow a few gulps of water from tin buckets. We did not know what to do first: Should we take a quick drink or relieve ourselves? There was not enough time to do both.

As a result of the intense heat in our cell, we were all extremely thirsty. My cellmates were very depressed, and their spirits continued to drop. I, too, was in a melancholy state of mind. The guards' harsh treatment of us spoke volumes.

Several of us felt that it would be better if the Germans had decided to kill us all at once, instead of the lethal combination of hunger, thirst, and uncertainty about the future, which would cause us all to die a slow and painful death.

Not for one second did I stop thinking about my mother's fate. Many thoughts ran through my mind. Where was she? Was she hungry? Had the fiendish Germans beaten her, God forbid? I also thought about the fate of my two younger sisters, who had been separated from us as we fled the German Army.

Tuesday, July 1

That day was not very different from the previous day. The only noticeable change was how weak and feeble we had all become. Our legs could barely hold us up, and it was as if our eyes had gone blind. We all felt faint and dizzy, and we wondered if those evil Germans hoped to starve us to death.

Wednesday, July 2

At 5:00 a.m., we were all taken to the prison courtyard. With great relief, I breathed in the fresh air to such an extent that my head began to spin. The German guards ordered us to line up in threes and to march directly to the center of town where we would clean the streets of the rubble from the bombings. As we walked, the Germans showered us with a relentless torrent of curses. In addition, they beat us mercilessly with their rifle butts and even kicked us with their hobnail boots.

For sixteen hours straight, we cleaned the streets and then returned to the prison where we each received two potatoes cooked in their peels and a bit of very watery soup. Nevertheless, that day was better than the previous day because at least we spent the entire day outside in the fresh air.

Hundreds of women holding babies waited along the sides of the road to meet their imprisoned husbands and brothers. Many women held packages of food for these men, but the German guards did not allow them to deliver the packages. However, some of the men managed to step out of line quickly and grab the food before the guards noticed.

When I returned to the prison, I happened to meet one of my neighbors, Yosef Katz, the shoemaker, whom I mentioned earlier. A thin Jew in his early forties, his years of hard work showed. He had regards for me from my mother and told me that her health was fine. She was living with his wife Sorel, their three small children, and other relatives at their family's house on Alleinaya Street in the center of town. Thanks to her hosts' generosity, my mother did not lack food; all she wanted was to meet me, even briefly. I was greatly relieved by my neighbor's welcome tidings.

Thursday, July 3

Before we were taken out to work early that morning, we were each given a piece of dry, moldy black bread and a cup of black coffee. Once again, the Nazi guards forced us to run down the street.

I looked toward the rows of women standing along the sides of the road and searched for my mother among them. This time, fortune smiled on me. After I had gone about fifty meters, I heard my mother's voice calling my name, "Chaim'l! Chaim'l!" I quickly stepped out of line and ran over to her. She gave me a small package, which contained a few freshly laundered summer undershirts and a pair of underpants. I managed to ask how she was doing, and after receiving a positive and encouraging response, I quickly rejoined the marchers.

Throughout that day, while hard at work clearing the streets of rubble, I did not stop thinking about my joyful encounter with my mother. It was as if the work had become easier, and the misery and torment of the prison did not exist. My only regret was that I had not thought to slip her a note with a few questions about her daily conditions. Thus, when I returned to my prison cell, I wrote a few lines on a scrap of paper, put the note in my pocket, and waited for an opportunity to give it to her.

That day, while I was working, I met a young man named Micha Kovlentz, about sixteen or seventeen years old, from the Lithuanian town of Zarasai,. Later, when we were lying next to each other in the cell, he told me that on Thursday, June 26, he had been the first one of the Jews traveling by train from Dvinsk to

Riga to witness the German paratroopers landing in the field next to the tracks. My mother and I had been on that same train, and he had volunteered to step out of the car to find out why we stopped moving. And then I remembered the incident.

As he described that fateful moment in our lives back there in the train car, I learned that Micha had noticed that the Latvian engineer and his assistant had suddenly brought the train to a halt to make a quick escape. Micha observed the German paratroopers storming the train. They then ordered the Jewish passengers to exit the cars and start marching northward toward Riga.

And now fate had reunited us. From then on, we became very good friends, and we decided to stick together and to make a real effort to avoid being separated, no matter what.

Friday, July 4

That morning, I did not see my mother. Work was particularly hard that day. We were forced to carry heavy wooden beams several kilometers while running quickly. I worked together with a black-bearded, short Jew, who was about fifty years old. Using all his strength, he carried the beams on his shoulders, as he ran as fast as he could.

When we reached our destination, the shore of the Dvina River near the iron bridge, he introduced himself to me. Before the war, he had lived in the city of Zarasai, where he served as a *rosh yeshiva* (yeshiva head) before the Soviets arrived in Lithuania. He told me that his heart was giving out and that he was getting weaker by the moment. Then he begged me to do everything in my power to ensure that he received a Jewish burial.

When we were finished hauling the wood, the Germans ordered us to carry heavy rocks uphill from the shore of the Dvina River. The Germans ordered us to run faster and even punched us, and that is when it happened. A certain Jew from Dvinsk, named Dondes, who apparently suffered from heart disease, suddenly stood still in his tracks. He was not strong enough to lug the heavy rocks. Immediately, a German shot him dead.

Throughout the day, they did not give us anything to eat or drink. Later that evening, when it started to get dark, the German soldiers used explosives to blow up a rock wall along the Dvina's southern shore. They wanted to build a new wooden bridge to replace the bridge which the Soviet Army had destroyed during their retreat. While the massive explosion was taking place, the Germans brought us through a large stone gate to a place, which would later be known as the Dvinsk ghetto. We continued to build the site from pieces of rock and did not stop working until 1:00 a.m. By the time the Germans brought us back to our prison cells, we were exhausted, dejected, and depressed.

Saturday, July 5

Once again, we left early in the morning to do hard labor, and as on the previous day, I did not see my mother. This concerned me greatly, and I became increasingly apprehensive about her fate.

That day, the work—clearing rubble from the streets—was somewhat easier. In the afternoon, we were brought to the same spot where we had labored the day before. To our surprise, before we started working, the Germans gave us a bit of soup in a bowl together with some black bread, and we were then given black coffee for dessert. We worked on building the new wooden bridge spanning the river. This time, there were neither specific cases of blatant abuse nor executions. My friend Micha and I were busy with the physically demanding work.

Sunday, July 6

Once again, we worked very hard that day. We carried cases of weapons that the Soviet Army had left behind in the warehouses in the fortress on the northern side of the Dvina during their retreat. The weather continued to be particularly hot, without a drop of rain. Yet, as we quickly hauled the heavy crates, in spite of the stifling heat, our German guards did not let us catch our breath or rest and did not give us any water to quench our thirst.

Meanwhile, not one of us ceased pondering the same perturbing and distressing questions: How long would our suffering continue? How much more could we endure? What did our oppressors have in mind to do to us?

Around that time, I unexpectedly found a German newspaper and read that the German Army had defeated an entire Soviet division near Bialystok and captured thousands of soldiers, together with their weapons and equipment. Furthermore, I learned that on the other fronts, the Germans were quickly advancing into western Russian territory. Although I did not believe everything I had read, I realized that the reports certainly contained elements of the truth. I became very upset and was unable to calm down.

Monday, July 7

Again we toiled very hard until evening. I always tried to work together with my friend Micha. This time, we worked at the fortress, loading buses and trucks with sacks of assorted materials that the Red Army had left behind during its hasty retreat. Although we were given something to eat in the afternoon, the fact that several days had elapsed since I had last seen my mother or received any information about her greatly disturbed me.

My friend Micha tried to console me and encourage me, "You're more fortunate than I am, because you still have a mother here in this city. But I don't know anything about my family or even if they're still alive." Every evening, Micha and I would make a point of lying next to each other on the floor of our prison cell after a day of hard labor. We would discuss all sorts of trivial incidents and events from the past to try and forget the present. In addition, we would dream about a better future until we fell asleep.

During one such conversation, Micha told me that if the hellish torment in prison did not abate and if the forced labor did not end, he preferred to die. In response, I tried to convince him that there is always hope and that one must never give up, especially when one is still young and in the prime of one's life. I told him that we still had the strength to survive in spite of our terrible suffering and misery, and therefore we must not despair. Also I noted that the German prison guards had increased our food rations. Perhaps, I mused, this was an indication that they needed us as a labor force in their war against the Soviets.

Tuesday, July 8

Once again, we were sent to the fortress for hard labor. Luckily, Micha worked next to me throughout the day. We cleaned and organized the filthy, garbage-strewn barracks, which had been abruptly abandoned by the Soviet Army. German companies were to occupy the barracks in their stead. As we toiled, the Germans spurred us to finish the task as soon as possible because the German companies were supposed to arrive the very next day.

To our great surprise, we were given hot food for lunch straight from the soldiers' kitchen, including a significantly larger portion of bread. And when we returned to our prison cells, we were given delicious pea soup with bread and black coffee. Moreover, in stark contrast to the other days, we were permitted to walk around the corridors. Usually, immediately after we had eaten, the guards shoved us back into our cells, as they yelled and cursed at us.

Nevertheless we could not enjoy our meal. After completing the day's labor, a group of Jews returned to their cells with extremely unwelcome tidings: One of them told us that a German officer had secretly whispered into his ear that the very next day all the Jews in the prison were to be executed. In addition, a second Jew stated that he was one of a large group of Jews who had been ordered by the Germans to dig a large pit in the garden behind the prison. The Jews had been severely beaten and punched in order to induce them to work quickly and finish digging the long, deep pit. We were stunned and devastated by these horrifying reports. Every Jewish prisoner spent that evening in shock.

Micha and I heard other news as well. A number of Jews had not been taken to work that day, and they related that several Jews had tried to look out the barred windows, which did not have a wooden covering. Immediately, the cruel German guards shot at them through the prison windows, and Bash, a Jewish engineer from Kovno, was killed.

Our hearts trembled. We all realized that death was imminent and that our lives hung in the balance. No one could fall asleep that night; we all spent the night tossing and turning.

Wednesday, July 9

At about 4:00 a.m., the skies were clear, and the sun beamed down from above. After hearing the cheerless tidings of the day before, we all yearned to be outside of the prison walls already. But what was going on here? The German guards were not coming to call us to work! Our hearts were still pounding from yesterday's news. Did that have something to do with this morning's events? The emotional tension increased; it seemed as if an eternity had elapsed. To make matters worse, our cells were unlocked and were, in fact, wide open. This seemed particularly ominous.

Suddenly, a Jew stood before us, visibly shaken and distraught. He told us that, with his own eyes, he had looked out the bathroom window and saw the Germans and the Latvians, armed with rifles and pistols, leading twenty-one Jews, in rows of three, toward the garden behind the prison. When we heard the Jew's terrible words, we all became paralyzed with fright. However, a few minutes later, when we heard rifle shots ring out from the same direction where the first victims had been led, a loud, mournful cry erupted from everyone's lips.

I ran over to the window and looked out. With my own eyes, I saw a new company of Jews being taken to their execution. The company included two brothers from Kovno, who had found shelter in the Latvian family's home, together with my mother and me, before we went to the market square. I also saw Yosef Katz, the shoemaker from Utian, and Shaltoffer, the tailor from Zarasai, and his two sons. Shaltoffer and I had met on the way to Dvinsk, when he was with his wife, daughter, and two sons. Now, he marched at the front of the group, embracing his sons, who walked on either side of him, with downcast eyes. I also saw that the group of condemned men included a certain young man, about my age, from Vilkomir, Lithuania. We had worked together, painting a school in Vilkomir for a full month, before the war erupted on September 1, 1939. My younger brother Moshe, of blessed memory, who died nine months later of tuberculosis, had worked with us, too.

The armed Latvians who surrounded the group had rifles and were wearing uniforms of the Aizsargs, a fascist Latvian organization founded before the Soviets arrived in Latvia. They were being particularly cruel to the Jews who knew them from Dvinsk. The Latvians beat them with their rifles and hurried the entire group forward to the entrance of the "garden of death."

And once again, we heard shots ring out from the same direction. Thus began the process of slaughtering the Jews whom the Germans had imprisoned in the Dvinsk prison.

Meanwhile, petrified and stunned, those of us in the cells on the third floor lost all concept of time. We started to say goodbye to each other and kissed even those Jews whom we had not known before. We resembled small children—infants—and we cried bitterly, as we wondered: Why?

"Yes, my dear brothers," one Jew addressed the crowd in an emotional voice. "We are being killed, not because of anything we have done but *al Kiddush Hashem* (the Sanctification of God's Name). We are being put to death only because we are Jews. But our spilled blood will scream and demand a great retribution!" The man said exactly what we had all been feeling and shouting. Someone told us that the speaker was the renowned actor Rudolf Zaslavski. We wandered around the third floor and awaited our turn, because the executions did not cease for a minute.

My friend Micha and I kissed each other emotionally and held hands.

"Are you afraid of death?" I asked him.

"No, not at all," he replied. "I look forward to dying, to being liberated from this terrible suffering."

When he asked me the same question, I also answered, "No." However, in my heart, I reflected that I was too young to die. I still hoped that I would remain alive and that I would also be privileged to see vengeance wreaked upon my people's murderers, the evil Germans.

After the killers had emptied the two lower floors of Jewish prisoners, we knew that the same process and the same end awaited us as well. Suddenly, we heard quick steps coming from the stairwell. The entrance door to the third floor creaked open, and a tall German with the features of an assassin, dressed in a Gestapo uniform, stood on the threshold. His eyes burned with bloodthirsty rage. He roared, "*Alle mit alles was ihr habt RAHS!*" ("All of you, with everything you have, GET OUT NOW!") When we heard the orders, we started to run, like frightened sheep, toward the prison's courtyard where the armed Latvian guards were waiting for us. The Gestapo division that had supervised the bloodbath quickly organized a group of twenty-one Jews, including us. We stood in rows of three. Micha and I held hands tightly. To our right and left, the Latvians marched in their Aizsargs uniforms. When the Gestapo officers ordered our group forward, the armed Latvian guards prodded us onward with shouts and curses.

Although the sun shone brightly, our eyes could see no light. Micha and I continued to hold hands. With my left hand, I started to tear the shirt I wore under my jacket, but a Latvian guard noticed what I was doing and dealt me a stunning blow with his rifle. I barely felt the pain; all I could think about was what was about to happen. I stopped tearing my shirt and let go of Micha's hand, lest the guard beat me again. When we reached the iron gate of the garden from which the shots had rung out—about one hundred meters from the entrance to the prison—our group was ordered to halt. I realized that the game was just about up. Another twenty steps on the other side of the gate, and then it was all over.

My brain froze. There was no question what awaited us. I saw four Latvians in Aizsargs uniforms. They were the firing squad, and they stood and waited for the order to fire. Twice, four Jews were taken from our group, and after each round of shots, they fell into the pit. Our turn was rapidly approaching.

But, then, a Latvian officer, who stood off to the side, gave a new order in Latvian. I understood only one word: *atpakal* (return or *atgal* in Lithuanian). The firing squad ceased firing, and the rest of our group was ordered to run into the park. We were given spades and ordered to hurry and cover the long pit, which was filled with our brothers' bodies.

A quick peek revealed that German soldiers or members of the Gestapo were standing near the fence, a few dozen meters away from us, filming the executions and the mass grave being filled with dirt by the victims themselves.

The firing squad was replaced by uniformed members of the Gestapo. They selected two men from our group and gave them a large sack filled with chlorine. They were then forced to descend into the giant grave to spread the chlorine over the still-writhing bodies.

As I shoveled the dust and sand into the grave, one thought went through my mind: If I were to be saved from these German murderers, my duty would be to report everything that my eyes had seen and everything that had happened to me in the Dvinsk prison.

Suddenly, one of the Germans hit me hard. He wanted me to pick up the pace of filling and sealing the giant grave. I heard other Jews from our group who were not working as quickly as the

Germans wished scream out in agony as well. *"Hinlegen!"* A tall German, with a murderous look in his eyes, ordered one of the Jews to lie face down on top of the bodies. The German bent down slightly, aimed his pistol directly at the victim's head, and fired a single bullet. The prone Jew lay motionless.

The entire execution took place right before my eyes. After the German returned his pistol to its holster, he once again started shouting at us to work faster. Once the pit was filled, the Latvian guards, who were waiting on the side for further instructions from the Germans, took us back inside the prison.

There is one more detail that I wish to add. While we were shoveling the dirt over the Jewish victims' bodies, the Gestapo men, who had ordered us to work quickly, acted as if they wanted to justify their atrocities and offered the following "explanation": The Fuhrer, they said, was the mastermind behind the annihilation of the Jews in every European country occupied by the Germans, and they were only following his orders.

This time, we were sent to the prison's ground floor; the upper floors were now empty. Later I learned that when our group had marched toward the garden to face the firing squad, other groups were behind us. Fate had temporarily smiled on them as well, and they, too, were brought back into the prison cells on the first floor. All of those who had returned to prison were now in the cells on the ground floor.

I did not see my friend Micha again.

We seemed to have been granted a temporary reprieve from death. The giant pit, which had been dug the day before in order to bury every one of the Jewish prisoners, could not hold all the bodies. Well aware of what was going on, we had no hope, no glimmer of light that we would be spared the terrible fate that still awaited us.

In my cell, there was another man from Utian, named Laibel Katz, whose family had lived on our street. He told me that he had moved from Utian to Dvinsk, where he had worked as a *shochet* (a ritual slaughterer). In light of our desperate situation, he and several other devout Jews recited chapters from the Book of Psalms. They beseeched the Master of the Universe to perform a miracle and save our lives.

We had neither food nor drink, but we were not even thinking about that. I was focusing on trying to figure out a hiding place where the German oppressors would not be able to find me. After all, I no longer had anything to lose.

As I looked around me, I noticed a stove at the end of the corridor, not far from the door, because our cell door was wide open. I wondered if I could somehow sneak into the oven without anyone seeing, and then I could hide inside temporarily. Obviously, it was not an ideal solution, but since it was the best I could come up with under the circumstances, I decided to go for it. Not for one minute did I stop thinking about my idea.

Late this afternoon, five men, including Laibel Katz, were led out of our cell and informed that they were being sent to labor. Later, only two of them returned to our cell. They said that they had been ordered to dig a grave behind the prison and then bury several Jews who had been shot to death in the city that day.

However, the bloodthirsty Latvian guards also killed three of our five Jewish cellmates who had been sent to "work." Laibel Katz was one of the three victims.

At about 5:00 or 6:00, all the Jews were led out the menacing iron gate and forced to dig a pit for themselves. We expected this to happen because the murderers wanted to ensure that there would be no living witnesses to their atrocities. The German Gestapo men ordered one group of Jews to run back and forth, nonstop, for several hours, on top of the giant pit containing the victims who had been killed that day. The rest of the Jews were divided into two groups. While one group dug our own grave, the other group was allowed to rest for a few minutes. Thus, we dug in turns. The lumps of earth covering the dead continued to shake even after our men stopped running.

While we were digging and running, the Gestapo men abused us mercilessly and incessantly. They shot and killed any Jew who seemed to tire and grow weak from the hard labor. When one man began to sob and beg the Germans not to shoot him, they ordered him to climb up to the pit's opening. With great difficulty, the poor Jew reached the opening, and then a sadistic German shoved him into the pit. This happened several times, and the German continued to taunt and torment the Jew. The other Gestapo men seemed to derive great enjoyment from the spectacle.

The Germans then turned to an elderly, bearded Jew and asked him how old he was. When he told them that he was sixty years old, they replied, "You've lived long enough," and shot him to death.

Another Jew told the Gestapo men that he had served in the German Army during World War I, but they immediately responded, "But you are a Jew!" They gave the same response to a young Jew in his twenties, who had been a soldier in the Soviet Army when the war had broken out, although he insisted that he had stopped fighting the Germans and had been taken prisoner by them.

Once again, the Germans justified their actions, as they had done that morning, when we covered the bodies with dirt. The Gestapo men declared that they were just following Hitler's orders to annihilate European Jewry.

In order to succeed with my plan to find a temporary hiding place inside the prison, I asked one of the Jews in my group to help me. His name was Shmuel "Shmulke" Peletz from Yanova, Lithuania, and he was about my age. I spoke to him in Lithuanian because I did not want the others to understand. I was well aware of the fact that only a minuscule number of young men could risk hiding inside the prison, if and when we would be led back inside. There was almost no chance that my plan would work, but I told myself that we had to try.

As it turned out, Shmuel shared my plan with two of his friends from Yanova—Efraim "Efroyke" or "Froyke" Milner, who was about nineteen, and Yeshayahu "Shayke" Eivensky, seventeen. With some hesitation, they agreed to cooperate because the plan had given them a glimmer of hope.

By the time we finished digging the pit, darkness had fallen. The Gestapo guards returned us to our cells on the ground floor and left the cell doors open, but they closed the main door that led to the railway garden. An armed guard stood near the entrance door on the other side of the long corridor. We could not see his face or his uniform because he was too far away, but that did not concern us then.

The four of us stood next to each other, anxiously waiting for a chance to execute our plans in front of the other Jews, who were aware of what was to happen to them the following morning. We stood with our backs to the stove in the corridor, and, with guarded expressions on our faces, we looked at our longsuffering brothers and watched how they responded to the bleak circumstances. Inside, our hearts cried for their bitter fates. They roamed the corridor, hopeless and desperate. They shook hands and kissed each other goodbye, as they had done the previous morning on the third floor.

When I showed my three new friends my designated hiding place behind the stove, they decided and I agreed that when people were still walking around the corridor, it would be impossible to hide there. Instead, we would have to seek a better and more appropriate hiding place. Luckily, such an opportunity immediately presented itself.

When all the Jews entered the cells on both sides of the corridor and the guard turned his back, the four of us quickly ran into the prison guards' room. Fortunately, the door was open, and the key was on the inside. A young man from Dvinsk, who was about thirty years old, noticed us running and joined us.

The room was square, about sixteen meters on each side. A window, which was about a square meter, overlooked the courtyard. (The window faced the door.) On the left, there were wooden shelves with various tools. On the right, about a meter and a half from the wall opposite the window, near the wall adjoining the next cell, there was a rather wide and tall stove. In the corner between the stove and the wall, thick winter blankets were thrown haphazardly on the floor.

The four of us from Lithuania hid under the blankets. However, the Jew from Dvinsk could not join us because he suffered from asthma. Thus, he remained next to the pile of blankets. A few minutes later, he started to cough. We told him that if he stayed in the room, none of us stood a chance; therefore, he soon left the room.

One of us—I believe it was Shayke—had a few dried sweets, which he had received from another man from Yanova shortly before we went to hide. The man had said to him, "I think you're planning something. So, take this. It might help…" As we lay there under the blankets, dividing the sweets among us really did help us a bit.

We recognized that the discomfort of lying under the blankets for such a long period of time was well worth the chance of staying alive, even for a short time. Not one of us slept a wink that night.

At dawn, we could hear the rest of the Jewish prisoners being led to their deaths in the garden. Since we were only a few steps away, we could hear everything quite clearly: the guards' shouts, the prisoners' screams, and, several minutes later, the shots. We knew that at that moment our friends were falling into the ditches, which we all had dug with our own hands the day before.

And, then, silence. The silence of a graveyard.

Thus, we became the sole Jewish survivors of the huge crowd that had been brought to the Dvinsk prison on June 29!

During those brief moments after the shootings, I realized that each and every second that we were still alive was a blessed gift. In the afternoon, we looked out the window and saw a large group of Jewish women marching with their children. We were able to exchange a few words with them, and we asked them where were they coming from and who they were. They told us that most of them were from Lithuania, and although they had tried to escape, the Nazis had caught up with them near the Soviet border. Later, I learned that there were about nine hundred in their group. After spending an entire day in the prison courtyard without food or drink, they were murdered the next morning in Dvinsk's "Yellow Sands" area.

Throughout the day, jailers entered and exited the room where we were still hiding and took several items off the shelves. Every time they came in, our hearts nearly stopped.

Meanwhile, we held on to the key. In the evening, we were terrified when the door opened. We heard voices speaking German, and we realized that a number of Germans had come into the room to look for boots. Our hearts pounded as they searched and stepped on our heads under the blankets. Death seemed to loom near, and we held our breaths until the Germans left the room.

The most frightening moment occurred when a German, who was standing on the pile of blankets, started to lift some of the blankets. But fortunately, he stopped when his friend said to him, "Stop looking. We definitely won't find anything good here." With a few choice curses, they left the room.

When the Germans walked out and locked the door behind them with a key, we felt much better and breathed a tremendous sigh of relief. We started to plan a way out of the room. After all, the unyielding strain and pressure was taking its toll on us. Each of us was immersed in his own thoughts, as we tried to figure out where we could go. Finally, we concluded that we had to leave that room, no matter the risk, either that night or the following night. We knew we had to act before sunrise.

Since we were all very tense, we felt that it was better to take some time to calm our nerves. Then, under the cover of darkness, we could start to implement our audacious plan, which had little chance of succeeding. Once again, we realized that we had no other options, and we agreed to go ahead with the plan. We would use one of the heavy tools on the shelf to kill the guard standing at the end of the corridor.

We understood that even if we managed to kill the guard, there was still a good chance that the Germans would notice and start shooting from the prison's watchtowers. Yet, we felt that if at least one of us got out alive, it was worth making the attempt.

The next day, before noon, we heard Jews talking in the corridor outside our door. Apparently, they were new arrivals because, until that moment, there did not seem to be anyone there.

One of us took off his blankets, approached the door, and asked the men, who were speaking Yiddish, if there were any guards in the area. We hoped that we would be able to open the door, step into the corridor, and join the men. However, before they had a chance to respond, the sentry at the end of the corridor bellowed menacingly. He had noticed from afar that a group of Jews was crowded near the door to our room. When he entered the room and saw that it was empty, he began pulling the blankets off our heads and discovered us. He immediately grabbed a heavy rope from one of the shelves and ordered us to leave the room. As we left, he delivered several severe and extremely painful blows to our heads and shoulders.

Once away from the sentry, we started to flee to the prison's upper floors. We had no idea why we did that because, after all, we knew that we would be caught eventually. Frantic, I ran up to the third floor and stepped into one of the rooms, where I found two captive Russian soldiers. My entrance and my menacing demeanor seemed to startle them. In Russian, I quickly explained that I was in great danger and needed a place to hide. The Latvian sentry was on my heels. I added that I had had no food or drink for three days and that I was extremely hungry and thirsty.

One of them gave me a piece of dry bread, and the other one offered his canteen and allowed me to take a few sips. But then, once again, we heard shouts, this time from the third floor corridor. Impulsively, I dived under a wooden bed that belonged to one of the soldiers. However, moments later, the sentry found me and dragged me out from under the bed.

He punched me and threw me into the corridor where I found Shayke and Efroyke. The guards brought us down to the corridor outside the room where we had been hiding. They had not yet found Shmulke, who had gone into a room holding Russian prisoners of war. When the sentry entered the room, Shmulke claimed that he was one of the Russian prisoners, but when the guards discovered that he was Jewish, they brought him back to us.

The four of us were forced to stand against the wall, as the sentry beat each of us viciously all over our upper body, including our head, with a heavy rope, even before we had recovered from the previous beatings. Meanwhile, two Germans, apparently from the Gestapo, arrived and watched with great relish as the sentry ordered us to remove our shirts, lie face down on the ground, and spread our arms and legs. He then brandished his heavy rope and struck us even harder, all the while yelling in Russian, "Will you run away?" And we whimpered in response, "No, we won't run away!"

Eventually, he tired of the sport and sent us each to different cells. In my cell, I spoke to the newly arrived Jews. I told them everything that had happened to us over the past few days, and they could not believe their ears. They gave me some food, a shirt, and a hat, lest I be recognized, God forbid.

Fortunately, both the Germans and the Latvian sentries believed that we were part of the new group of Jews because they assumed that the previous group had all been killed. Therefore, the search was called off. In fact, in the evening, the same sentry came into the room and asked if any of the four Jews he had beaten was present. When he was told that we were not, he moved on to the next cell.

We were not given any food until Monday, July 14, in the afternoon. In the meantime, we were allowed only occasional sips of water to quench our thirst. But on that Monday, the guards placed a large pot of barley soup in the corridor. Everyone rushed over and, like hungry wolves, waited for their portions. The person serving up the soup was a tall, heavyset man named Kadishvitz, from Dvinsk, who in the past had been known as a communist.

On Tuesday, July 15, in the afternoon, we again were given soup from that large pot. Toward evening, the Gestapo guards came to our corridor and organized a "selection"—separating Jews with occupations from those with so-called "liberal professions." I declared that I had painted houses and signs, and they immediately directed me to one of the cells on the right side of the corridor. All the Jews with liberal professions were sent to the cells on the corridor's left side. The doors to those cells were then shut, and early the next morning, July 16, those Jews were led to the infamous "garden of death" and shot to death. The victims included many of Dvinsk's leading Jewish scholars and intellectuals.

At 8:00 a.m., we were taken to load coal onto freight trains and to do other types of backbreaking physical labor. That day, each worker received about two hundred grams of dried bread and about half a liter of watery soup in addition to black coffee, without sugar, twice during the day.

I hoped and believed that I would get some information about my mother and her wellbeing that day, but I was disappointed to hear no news. Mainly, I wanted to send her a sign, a hint, that I was still alive. She undoubtedly had heard about the fate of the first Jews that were brought to the Dvinsk prison. After all, the murders were carried out in broad daylight in the middle of the city.

Every morning, from Thursday, July 17, until Sunday, July 27, between 5:30–6:30, they would drag Jews out of their cells into the corridor, beat them viciously, and finally lead them to their deaths. It was hard to forget the victims' screams followed by the sounds of the shootings. They continued to reverberate in our ears throughout the day.

Feigelson, a certain distinguished and venerable Jew from Dvinsk, remains etched in my memory. Elderly and with a beard, he raised his hands and, crying bitterly like a child, he prayed to God to have mercy on his life.

One day, Froyke Milner, one of the three young men from Yanova who had hidden with me, was taken from the prison with nine other guys to forced labor somewhere in the city. Not one of them returned.

Froyke was a good-looking, young man with black, curly hair. Even when times were rough, he never stopped smiling. According to what we heard, their group was supposed to bury ten German soldiers who had died of their wounds in the city's military hospital. Apparently, after the Jews finished their task, they were shot. Only one of their group, Shmarke Nemiyot, who was also from Yanova, managed to escape. He eventually joined the partisans and fought against the Germans with great valor. But while fighting against a German supply company, he was shot to death by his Russian commander. The Russian commanders were also filled with a profound hatred for their comrades, the Jewish fighters.

I would often meet my friends, Shayke and Shmulke, from Yanova, in prison. But then one day, they were both taken to work as carpenters in what was to become the ghetto; fortunately for them, they never returned to Dvinsk prison.

Meanwhile, when I was working with other Jews clearing rubble from the streets of Dvinsk, I happened to meet a Jewish woman from Utian, who had regards for me from my mother. This encouraged me greatly and I felt almost energized. The next day, a young man from Dvinsk brought me a short handwritten note from my mother. She asked that I write back with a quick update about my health, but I had no chance to do so.

During my final two days in Dvinsk prison, I was assigned to the German Military Field Headquarters, which was located in the middle of Dvinsk, in the building that had served as the district courthouse before the war. I worked as an assistant to a Jewish sign painter from Dvinsk named Tuviah Luvy. He was a nice man in his thirties, short, dark, and very talented, and I had a lot to learn from him. His main assistant was Betzalel Elrin, who was about the same age and was also from Dvinsk. Betzalel had great public relations skills and found a way to approach the German major, who made sure that all the Jewish workers had enough food. Also, two brothers from Dvinsk, Moshe and Yaakov Megram, and several other Jews from Dvinsk worked there as well. In addition, one of the other sign painters was a pleasant fellow from Mariampol, Lithuania, named Moshe Averov. A friendly and extremely talented man, he was about twenty-six years old and had studied biology at the University of Kovno. During the two days that I worked with that team, I did not have a chance to get to know everyone very well.

At the end of the second day, when I returned to the accursed prison, I sensed that there had been a change. Throughout the day, I had heard from a number of different people that all the Jews of Dvinsk and its environs were being brought to the southern side of the Dvina River to the ancient fortress, which the Latvian cavalry had used as stables and residences before the Soviets arrived. And the site was now known as the ghetto.

As soon as we arrived back at the prison, the Latvian guards insisted that we quickly drink our unsweetened black coffee and head to the prison courtyard. Is it possible, I wondered, that we will get out of here alive?

In the courtyard, we saw Jewish women with their small children and assorted bundles and parcels in their arms, walking and visibly distraught. When we asked them where they had come from, they explained that Latvian guards had gathered them from the roads around Dvinsk and brought them to the prison. Together with us men, the entire group numbered about two hundred men, women, and children.

We were led out of the courtyard and then turned left on the main road, heading south. As we walked, the Latvian guards forced us to hurry as they cursed and reviled us. When we men tried to take the heavy parcels that the women were struggling to hold in their arms or carry on their shoulders, the guards grabbed the packages and tossed them on the sides of the road.

After we crossed the iron bridge that spanned the Dvina River, we turned right and came to an ancient, semicircular fortress with high, stone walls. To the left of the tall entrance gate, which had a rounded top, was a sign with the German inscription, *"Ghetto Dünaburg"* ("The Dvinsk Ghetto"). Before we entered the gate, our armed escorts left. The armed guards at the gate, who were also Latvian, ordered us to enter the ghetto. We all went off in different directions to search for our relatives.

This all took place on the evening of Monday, July 29, 1941, and marked the beginning of a new stage of my suffering and torment under the cruel Nazi regime.

CHAPTER THREE:

The Dvinsk Ghetto

As I searched for my mother, I wandered among the Jewish crowds in the ghetto's packed circular courtyard, which surrounded the ancient two-story building. I figured that she had already lost hope that I was still alive, because everyone knew what had happened to the Jews who had been taken to the prison on Sunday, June 29.

And then, suddenly, our eyes met. Hugs, kisses, and tears of joy. We were so excited that we could not speak. When we had calmed down a bit, my mother took my hand and led me to her quarters in the ghetto.

She had arrived only three days earlier, together with Efraim Kobb from Utian, his wife, their daughter, their daughter-in-law, his sisters and their children who lived elsewhere in the ghetto, and another woman from Dvinsk, Mrs. Zilberman. My mother explained that this dear family had adopted her immediately after we were separated in the city square on that fateful Sunday. Both their sons, one married, had been murdered in cold blood at the prison.

My mother introduced me to them with the Yiddish words, "*Ich hob a gefunenem zun!*" ("I have found my son!") Her eyes beamed with happiness.

She told me that she worked in a military kitchen in the city with these four women, and, compared to many of the ghetto's inhabitants, they were satisfied. The physical work in the kitchen was tolerable, and they did not lack food. I remembered that when I walked with my mother to her room and saw the terrible suffering of the throngs of people lying in every corner and thoroughfare, I thought that it was fortunate that my mother had at least found work and belonged to a supportive group of nice women. I remained in their room for a while, and we asked each other all sorts of questions. But we did not discuss the current conditions in the ghetto. They spoke for themselves. And we knew that we faced an intractable struggle against a cruel fate.

I kissed my mother good night and then went to find a place to sleep among the men. After passing through several dark halls, I lay down, in my clothes, on some wooden benches, and due to sheer exhaustion and tension, I fell asleep.

In the morning at about 7:00, before my mother left for work with her group, she gave me a slice of bread, which she had saved from the previous day. Since I was unemployed that day in the ghetto, I quickly took in the appalling state of the ghetto's Jewish inhabitants. By the light of day, the scene was even more shocking than the night before. It is impossible to describe the strange maelstrom in which I encountered the masses of starving, humiliated Jews, who had lost everything, including hope. Using whatever strength they had left, these people fought a day-to-day war of survival against the heinous German and Latvian overlords.

I learned that the ghetto had been established by German decree on July 26. All the Jews in Dvinsk and the surrounding area, together with the Lithuanian Jewish refugees who had not managed to escape the Nazi oppressors, were brought to the ghetto. The Jews were allowed to bring a few basic necessities with them, as much as they were able to carry. I was told that during the move from the city to the ghetto, the wretched convoy of humanity was several kilometers long and included the elderly, the handicapped, pregnant women, children, teenagers, and any men who had not been taken away. Other victims on that dreadful Sunday had already filled the prison.

Meanwhile, the various Latvian nationals jumped at the chance to plunder the homes that the Jews were forced to leave behind together with all their worldly possessions.

As the Jews made their way on foot to the ghetto, the Latvian guards cursed, reviled and even beat them, and the city's non-Jewish residents stood along the streets and roads and watched their former neighbors with indifference and even outright gratification. The ghetto's new residents, who settled into the dark stables that the Latvian cavalry had used to house their horses before the Soviets arrived, suffered from terrible overcrowding, unsanitary conditions, and starvation.

The babies had no milk, the older children begged for food, and the adults suffered in silence. At midday, there was a bit of watery soup made of rotten cabbage mixed with maggots. Whoever was still able to stand in line, in spite of the heat and the crowds, received some soup, but many people were too weak to reach the queue.

At 6:00 p.m., my mother returned from work with the four women who worked with her, and in her hands, she carried a basket of food for me! The basket, covered with a towel to keep the food warm, held fried potatoes and bread! As I ate, my mother watched me with unconcealed pleasure, and she made sure that I had a hot drink after I had finished eating. She boiled the water in a small metal pot over two bricks in the sandy area behind the ghetto wall. The ghetto's Jews were allowed to go there. My mother did not touch the food herself. She claimed that she had eaten at work. I had to believe her, but in my heart I wondered if she was really telling the truth. Maybe she just said that because she did not want me to feel guilty. Who can penetrate a mother's soul?

Every evening, after work—for nearly three weeks in a row— my mother would bring me food and hot water. I never once saw her eat anything herself. When I had finished my meal, including the hot water, I would find an empty corner where my mother and I could sit and talk. We would discuss the current outlook in the ghetto. Mainly, I tried to convince her not to trust the Germans. After all, I had learned from bitter experience in prison. They told us that we were being sent to "work," but the final outcome was very different. In addition, my mother would tell me that she was worried about Chaya and Sarah, who had been separated from us, but we tried to be optimistic about their fate. Maybe they were in a better place. Maybe. We also spoke about our concerns about the fate of our relatives, except those who had managed to flee the Nazi horrors, who were scattered among the various towns in eastern Lithuania. And we worried about the fate of Lithuanian Jewry in general.

One day, my mother reminded me that the 17th of Tamuz would mark her forty-third birthday. It occurred to me that my mother was still very young!

After remaining in the ghetto for several days, I managed to join a labor group that worked for the Germans in the citadel on the northwestern side of the Dvina River. Our group was charged with sorting the clothes of the Red Army's officers and soldiers. The work, which lasted about ten days, was not particularly difficult. They did not rush us, and once a day, we were given bread and nourishing soup. Every day, I would return to the ghetto with some tobacco, which I found among the uniforms, and then trade it for bread or other food with people who smoked but had no access to tobacco where they worked.

My mother praised me for taking the initiative. "Something about you has recently changed, my son," she noted. "Apparently, life teaches a person how to get through tough times." I had already told her how my life and the lives of three other young men were saved from certain death in prison, thanks to my initiative.

From the time the Gestapo and the SD (the security forces), together with their collaborators—the Latvian commandant and police—founded the ghetto, its Jewish inhabitants received all sorts of orders almost daily. Yet, not all the orders reached the inhabitants' ears. The orders were transmitted via the *Kommitet* (literally, "committee"), whom the German used to carry out their evil plans. Misha Movshenzon, a former engineer, headed the Kommitet with the help of his wife, Grunya. The Germans referred to him as the "*Oberjude.*" Other members of the Kommitet included Galpern and his wife; Dr. Danman and his wife, Dr. Vafsi, a pediatrician, and his wife; and Mrs. Landau, who oversaw the food depot and later also the factories in the ghetto. Pasternak, a Jew from Kraslava, was in charge of the Jewish policemen. In addition, the two Diament brothers, Nachum Pressman and his sons, Feigin, and several other people worked for the Kommitet.

The first order was to wear a yellow Star of David, made of cloth, on one's chest and back. Also, those who worked outside the ghetto were forbidden to walk on the city's sidewalks. We were also forbidden to enter any homes, stores, restaurants, or the market to ensure we avoid contact with non-Jews. Even purchasing a newspaper at a kiosk was punishable by death.

The Kommitet members committed many sins against their Jewish brothers, in terms of food distribution, work, and most importantly, the selections. Sorting the Jews in accordance with the Germans' decrees: Who will live, and who will die? They thought that if they obeyed orders with distinction, they would be spared their brothers' terrible fates. And thus, they tried to carry out every order, even if their hearts and souls opposed it.

One such order was to compile a list of the ghetto's inhabitants, according to place of residence prior to the German invasion. These lists enabled the Germans to identify those who were not from Dvinsk—i.e., the Jews who had fled Lithuania toward the Soviet border and had been stranded in Dvinsk or the surrounding area before being transferred to the ghetto. This group of refugees was added to a separate list with one objective: annihilation.

My mother found a solution for us with respect to the aforementioned registration. Since she worked together with a group of local women, who had lived in Dvinsk before the war, she learned from them that Alleinaya Street had been bombed and almost completely destroyed. Thus, we registered ourselves using a fictitious address on that street at a house number that no longer existed.

Before I continue to write about my mother's fate, I will briefly recount what I know and remember about the three aktions (mass killings), which took place in the ghetto.

I will begin with the first aktion:

On the evening of July 29, when I met my mother, we heard a rumor that the day before, high-ranking SD officials had selected approximately five hundred sick and elderly Jews. Supposedly, these Jews were to be transferred outside the city to a new camp with better conditions because the ghetto had become too crowded for them. However, the truth was that the following day, at sunrise, they were all shot to death in the Pogulyanka Forest. (This is the place where the train to Riga stopped, as I explained in Chapter One.) Once again, the Nazi murderers employed a ruse to entice their victims out of the ghetto.

The site of the murder was about six or seven kilometers away from the ghetto, behind the citadel on the right side of the street, which ran parallel to the Dvina River and led northward to Riga.

The second aktion, on August 2, occurred in the afternoon in the ghetto. Since many Jews from the towns surrounding Dvinsk had been brought to the ghetto the day before, and the ghetto had become extremely overcrowded, the Germans decided to reuse the same trick. Once again, the victims were promised that they were being taken to a less-crowded location. In order to lull suspicions, the victims were permitted to bring all their possessions so that they could begin "a new life," in the Germans' words. The Germans even sent Dr. Gurevitch, a well-known and popular physician from Dvinsk, along. He thought that this was an important mission and willingly joined his unfortunate brothers and sisters and their families.

However, as Dr. Gurevitch, the sole survivor of that massacre, later reported, one of the killers, who had been a former patient, recognized the doctor and saved his life. Yet, thousands were ignobly deceived and ensnared by the murderers' trap.

Later, in the Riga ghetto, Dr. Gurevitch shared details about the massacre of the province's Jews on August 2, with Jacob Rassen, the author of a book, which was published in New York in 1949. The following quote comes from him:

> "With my own eyes, I saw how the deceived Jews
> panicked when a heavy bombardment suddenly
> rained down upon them from every direction, and
> they started to drop into the pits, which had been
> prepared in advance. The murderers threw the half-

dead into them. At the end of the massacre, I saw that the earth, which had been poured over the victims, had risen. Among the province's men, there were a number who were physically and emotionally strong, who in desperation fell upon their murderers and managed, before they were shot, to drag some of them into the pit, as they strangled them with their hands.

"Several dozen murderers were also wounded by those heroes, even after they had been shot and every part of their bodies was covered in blood. I was an eyewitness, against my will and unable to offer any help whatsoever."

As he told his story, he cried bitterly.

Several days after the terrible massacre of the provincial Jews, once again the murderers arrived toward evening and ordered all of us to go outside and form lines. They announced that those who had left Lithuania and wished to return home would be transferred back to their original places of residence. Moreover, no harm would come to them, the murderers promised.

Several hundred Lithuanian refugees naively believed the Gestapo and stepped forward. The Lithuanian "returnees" were never heard from again. Once the selection was completed, my mother and I went back to our rooms with the feeling that we had done the right thing. I had managed to convince her not to believe the Gestapo's lies.

After the Lithuanian refugees were removed from the ghetto during the last aktion, there were about ten days of relative quiet. As was the case before the previous aktions, the mood in the ghetto was tense due to the uncertain future. Everyone feared that the murderers would resort to additional ruses in order to reduce the ghetto's population.

Meanwhile, my mother and I continued to work at the same jobs: She worked at the Feldpost military kitchen, and I worked for the Wehrmacht at the citadel, sorting Russian soldiers' clothing. As we worked at the uniform warehouses, my fellow workers and I discussed our future outlook. Some of us, myself included, allowed a faint note of cautious optimism to creep into our words. We believed that if we continued to work and help the Nazi war effort, perhaps we would be spared the bitter fate that awaited us all. Every one of us had a work permit that we had received from the German military.

On Saturday, August 16, my work at the citadel ended. I no longer had any work papers, which meant that my life was in danger.

On Sunday morning, August 17, I walked with my mother to the gate. After we said goodbye, she joined her coworkers. I remained standing near the gate, with a glimmer of hope in my heart that maybe she would be able to find work for me outside the ghetto. Yet, it was to no avail. I spent the day in the ghetto waiting, wandering about despondently, and trying to come up with an idea, until my mother returned from work with food for me.

From the time I arrived in the ghetto, I kept in touch with my two friends from Yanova—Shayke and Shmulke—who had hidden with me in prison. I was particularly close with Shayke, who was lucky enough to find his younger brother, Reuvke, who was about fifteen years old. One day, Shayke told me that he and Shmulke worked together as part of the same group in the city. They each had a work permit (known as a "*schein*" in German), which protected them, at least temporarily, against the aktions that threatened the lives of the ghetto's inhabitants. His only regret was that Reuvke had no regular work, and he was very concerned about his younger brother's fate.

After I finished eating, my mother and I discussed what was likely to take place the next day in the ghetto. Some of those who worked in the city had returned to the ghetto with ominous reports about the following day. Of course, my mother had reason to be afraid for me, because I had not worked since Saturday. I tried to calm her down by noting that I had experience handling life-threatening situations. However, I was not sure that I had managed to allay her fears because I myself was very concerned. Yet, when I said goodnight to my mother that evening, I realized that I had no choice but to try my luck the next day. Perhaps I would somehow find work in the city.

The next day, I accompanied my mother to the gate, and before we kissed each other goodbye, she warned me, "Chaim'l, in the event that you don't go to work, hide in the ghetto, and may you succeed!"

I had the same idea. Nevertheless, I stood with a fairly large group of people who hoped to go work in the city, and I waited anxiously for a miracle. Next to me stood a young man from Kraslava, which was located about thirty kilometers from Dvinsk. He told me that he had lost his entire family in the previous aktions. He was only seventeen years old and he wanted to stay alive. By profession, he was a carpenter, and he really hoped that a German contractor would come and offer him carpentry work or any other job, anything that would get him out of the ghetto.

As my friend Baruch Kwill and I stood there next to each other, tense and facing forward, two German soldiers approached us. When they asked if we had carpentry skills, we both answered, "Yes." I told myself that even if it was not professional, my friend Baruch would be able to direct me. We walked out of the gate with the two soldiers and felt much better. The main thing was that we were outside. I was not worried about my mother, because after all, she had a schein.

The soldiers brought us to the area between the Dvina River and the ghetto, which was on higher ground than the ghetto. We noticed a large group of Jews to the left of the soldiers' tent. The German soldiers had brought the entire group, which included women, middle-aged men, and even a small boy of about three or four with his mother.

It occurred to me that these two soldiers were doing something extraordinary in that cruel, inhumane time. They were saving Jewish lives! There was to be an aktion, and they were doing what they could until the mortal danger had passed. And in so doing, they were endangering their own young lives! Unbelievable!

We entered the soldiers' tent and asked about the carpentry work. They immediately responded that they had taken us out of the ghetto not only to work.

"First of all," they said, "we understand that you must be hungry. Sit down and eat, and then we'll see what's next."

They served us dishes of berries and cream as well as good-quality bread of the type given to soldiers in the German Army. In addition, they brought us sweetened coffee with milk and cake! We could not believe our eyes. Was it possible that there were still men in the German Army who cared for the unfortunate Jews?

We thanked them and stepped outside the tent with them. They led us to a partially disassembled wooden hut a few meters away. The soldiers gave us tools, such as a hammer and pliers, to take the rest of the hut apart. After completing the task, we were to sort the wooden boards and then straighten the nails and place them in a separate box.

We worked energetically and finished the work within a few hours. The soldiers asked us if we wanted to rest or to walk around. We chose the second option because we wanted to speak to our Jewish brothers and sisters.

We soon discovered that these Jews had arrived on the previous day. These Germans, whom the Jews referred to as "angels," had led them out of the ghetto because they knew that there was to be an aktion. According to the Jews, the Germans' sole objective was saving lives.

This group of Jews included a famous doctor from Dvinsk and his family. I cannot remember his name. The young, pretty woman with her three- or four-year-old son was married to Ben-Tzion Sheffer, a butcher from Dvinsk. I did not learn the others' names.

At around 3:00 p.m., the aktion began. It was all over by midnight.

I told the soldiers that my mother worked in the Feldpost's military kitchen and that she had the critical schein, which would protect her during the aktions. Yet, nevertheless, I started to feel some misgiving. I had an uneasy sense that her life was in danger after all, but I could not explain why. When I revealed my concerns to the two soldiers, they tried to calm me down.

Throughout that evening and night, I did not close my eyes. I was waiting for sunrise to return to the ghetto to make sure that nothing had happened to my mother. Sadly, there was no longer any need for my friend Baruch to rush back to the ghetto, but he still hoped that I would find my mother among the living. He understood how emotional I felt during those tense minutes and hours.

When the soldiers heard the shouts and the heartbreaking cries of the wretched people in the ghetto, they cursed the murderers and said that history would never forgive them for their despicable crimes. Like Baruch and I, they stayed awake all night. Several times, Baruch and I tried to lie down on the tent floor and get some sleep, but we were unable to do so, even though once the aktion ended, quiet prevailed from the direction of the ghetto.

I left the tent very early the next morning after thanking the benevolent soldiers who had saved our lives for all that they had done for us during our time of need. My friend Baruch stayed in the tent with them.

I ran to the ghetto, and, avoiding the gate, I headed straight to the room that my mother shared with her friends. One look at these women's stone-faced expressions, and it was clear that I no longer had any reason to go search for my mother. Yet, out of force of habit, I stepped out of the room to look for her there. Maybe she had gone to relieve herself or to wash her face.

But when I returned to the room, the women told me what had happened the day before. By the time they all had returned from work, at around 6:00 p.m. as usual, the aktion was going on in full force. When my mother saw the crowd of Jews on the left, she thought that she saw me standing among those hapless Jews and decided to join them. "If my son Chaim is not going to live, I have no reason to live either."

I did not know what to do with myself. How could I continue living when that which was most precious to me had been tragically lost? My poor mother, you took care of me with such devotion, every day throughout my entire life, until the bitter end!

The women tried to console me. They said that I was still young, that I still had my whole life ahead of me, and that I had the proven ability to survive. In the corner of the room where my mother would store the leftover food that she brought home from work, I found a few scraps of bread. I put the bread in my pocket and left the room. Hoping that someone would come looking for workers, even for one day, I headed toward the gate. Anything to escape the next death trap, which, according to several people, was scheduled for that day.

On my way to the gate, I saw Sorel Katz, our neighbor from Utian, who was walking with her three small children. I remembered that Sunday in the marketplace when she had told us that the Germans had taken her husband, Yosef the shoemaker, and that she expected him to return at the end of the workday. As it turned out, her husband was massacred together with the other Jews in prison.

I told her that I had lost my mother in the previous day's aktion, but she replied indifferently, "Chaim'l, you must know that yesterday was her turn and today, apparently, my children and I will go the same way. This is our fate. I can't look at these children anymore, how they're suffering and hungry. And I can't help them or myself."

I had no answer for her.

I then thought about Shayke, Shmulke, and Reuvke and wondered how they would cope with the day's anticipated aktion. As I stood near the gate, waiting for work, a group of men passed by on their way to their jobs on the outside. Reuvke was among them. He reached out his hand to me with a 100-ruble note and asked that I give it to his brother Shayke, in case he would never see him again. His words proved to be prophetic.

After waiting for a short while, I was surprised when someone came and offered me work. And who was my employer? The SD! Together with several other young men, who had also been waiting for work on the outside, I was taken to the city's SD headquarters, the vile murderers' nest, where they organized the aktions in the ghetto!

They told me to clean and oil the officers' bicycles and to shine their boots. Surprisingly, they treated me fairly decently and even gave me some delicious, nourishing soup, which contained a lot of vegetables, and bread. In the early afternoon, they took us back to the ghetto without giving us any papers showing that we worked for them.

At about 3:00, the aktion began. It was the second one in as many days! I noticed that the *very same senior officers whom I had served earlier that day* implemented the aktion. I recognized their faces.

As with the previous aktions, this one began with an order that all of the ghetto's inhabitants come outside and line up in the courtyard. Everyone was strained and tense. Documents were checked and then the orders were given. Who to the right and who to the left?

Instinctively, I tried to push my way to the back. A young redheaded woman, whom I did not recognize, noticed my apprehension and whispered, "Stand next to me, and I'll say that you're my brother." She had a schein in her hand. I calmed down somewhat and stood next to her, holding her hand as the murderers drew nearer.

One of them approached me. I remembered his face with its distinctive features very well. His cold and watery grey eyes conveyed complete indifference to everything that was happening around him. In the morning, he had told me what I needed to do for them and now he was asking me if I had a work permit. The young woman answered for me and said that I was her brother and that she had work. She showed him her schein. He let us go and moved on.

Thus, for the second time in two days, my life was spared. When the aktion was over, I thanked the woman who had saved me from the murderers and went to the large men's room, where I slept at night on the bare benches. I lay down on a bench in order to rest up from the tension and started thinking about all that I had witnessed during the aktion. Once again, the ghetto had been emptied of several thousands of its Jewish inhabitants, whose clothes and possessions were strewn everywhere.

I was awakened by the loud cries and heartbreaking sobs of a young man named Berke Kaplan, who was about seventeen years old and was my bunkmate. Tall and good-looking, he was from Dvinsk, and after he had calmed down somewhat, he told me that he had also lost his mother that day. I knew what he was going through. Like everyone else in the ghetto, we both understood that we were living on borrowed time.

After the second aktion, we learned that as the victims were marched over the bridge leading to the Pogulyanka Forest, they deliberately tore up their cash and destroyed their valuables so that the murderers would not be able to get their hands on them.

I went to check up on Shayke, his brother Reuvke, and Shmulke. Sadly, I learned that Reuvke, who had given me that 100-ruble note for his brother, was one of the victims of the second aktion on the previous day. I gave the money to Shayke. He was devastated by his younger brother's death. Reuvke had been the sole surviving member of their immediate family.

Later, I met Efraim Kobb from Utian as he was leaving the ghetto to go to work. He had already lost his two sons in prison, but he still had his wife, his daughter, his sister, and his daughter-in-law. His sister, Sorel Katz, whose husband had been murdered in prison, and her three children were killed during the most recent aktion. How had she foreseen this?

Efraim tried to comfort me, "After the last aktion, there are now many small children in the ghetto without their parents. You've become a man, and you can survive. Stay strong!"

In order to survive, I needed to find work, and one day, thanks to a certain Jew whom I knew from prison, I got a job as an assistant sign painter. The work was in the center of town, opposite the prison, in the elegant building that had served as the district courthouse before the war and was known as the *Ortskommandantur.* On the first day, when I reported to the German who hired me, I had to take a proficiency test.

In my group, which consisted of about eight men, there was only one top-notch sign painter. The rest were assorted tradesmen, who were given various jobs by the German officer, a major, who commanded the military unit based in the building. Our daily food rations were not bad, and we even had enough left over to bring back to the ghetto after we finished work at 6:00.

We all relied on the professionalism and skills of one man, Tuviah Luvy, a short, dark Jew from Dvinsk with alert eyes. About thirty years old, he prepared assorted road signs in German. Together with Moshe Ayerov, a twenty-six year old from Mariampol, who had studied biology at the University of Kovno before the war, I would help Tuviah prepare the tins for painting.

Moshe and I became very friendly. A brilliant, multitalented, and vivacious man, he had lost contact with his wife while fleeing Kovno. He loved music, jewelry-making, and acting. Like all of us, he hoped to get through the war in one piece. He would design jewelry for the German soldiers, who gave him food in return.

Tuviah had a wife and two small sons in the ghetto, and every evening they would wait for him to bring some food from the kitchen, which he was able to get thanks to his connection to the major. Since it was a very long walk to the ghetto, and because he was physically weak, I offered to help Tuviah carry the package of food.

Another member of our group, Elrin, from Dvinsk, also had non-Jewish connections and was thus able to supply his elderly father in the ghetto with food. The rest of us made do with the rations we received at work.

Occasionally, I was able to purchase, at great danger, a German newspaper. I knew that Leningrad was surrounded and that the front was moving closer to Moscow. There was no good news on the Ukrainian front, either. The Nazi Army had captured all the big cities: Kiev, Kharkov, and Odessa. Meanwhile, the optimists among us, myself included, still hoped that if the battles continued into winter, the attacking German Army would be halted; after all, that had been the fate of Napoleon's army in 1812.

Following the aktions of August 18 and 19, we heard no rumors about additional aktions during September and October. The ghetto's inhabitants relaxed a bit. They noted that many men and women were serving the German Army in the city, and they believed that this justified our continued existence. They thought that anyone possessing a schein was protected, as were all their relatives in the ghetto.

During this period, there were isolated incidents of capital punishment. Two women "broke" the law by trying to obtain a bit of food for their starving children and were put to death in public executions in the ghetto. As far as I can remember, the women's names were Meyerov and Gittleson.

We heard rumors that the Latvians had organized a military unit that would fight together with the Wehrmacht (the German Army). In return, they were asked to liquidate Dvinsk's ghetto.

In October, I had an unexpected surprise. One cold and rainy evening, as our group passed through the ghetto's entrance gate on our way back from work, I heard someone call my name repeatedly from a nearby wooden hut. Startled, I wondered who could have recognized me. I left my group and walked over to the hut. Before me, I saw two eyes peering out at me from a crack in the wall. The man's face was covered in a dark brown beard, and it was hard to determine his age. Initially, I did not recognize him. But when he stated his name—Motke from Aniksht, a town located some thirty-five kilometers from my hometown of Utian—I realized that he was my cousin. When I asked how I could help him, he said, "Bring me a blanket, so I can cover myself at night, because it's very cold."

I told myself that it would take more than a blanket to solve his problems, and I knew I had to act quickly if I was to gain his release from the hut. Thus, I turned to the Kommitet, which still had some authority, and said that the man who had been arrested on various charges was my cousin. I explained that I worked for a German military unit, and after showing them my work permit, I pleaded with them to release my cousin to my protection immediately. Apparently, my entreaties made an impression on them, because they decided to ask the Latvian commander of the ghetto to release him.

After embracing and kissing each other, my cousin and I went to my room. As he told me everything that had happened to him and his family—my family—the other men in the room gathered around and listened, with mouths agape. Obviously, before he started to speak, I gave him all the food and drink I had, and my neighbors also contributed whatever they could.

His story began when the Germans arrived in Aniksht and, with the help of the local Lithuanian collaborators, began persecuting the local Jews. Several times, my cousin managed to escape their bloodstained hands. However, he ultimately fell into their hands, after they had brutally murdered several hundred Jewish men in the nearby forest known as *Hauzenberg* (Rabbit Hill). In this particular instance, they brought a relatively small group of young men there. He knew them all by name, including a father and son. The murderers shoved the Jews into a pit, which had been prepared in advance, and fired.

Before the shooting began, my cousin covered his head with his right hand. Nevertheless, two bullets hit him, one in his right arm and one in his lower body. Believing that their victims were all dead, the murderers left before nightfall. In spite of his wounds, my cousin managed, with great effort, to climb out of the pit, with the moans of the dying ringing in his ears.

The family of a Lithuanian girl, whose friendship with my cousin predated the Soviet arrival in Lithuania, lived near the forest. Her name was Verute Masionaite. She and my cousin used to dance together, and then he would occasionally escort her home. Summoning his courage, he walked straight to her house but was afraid to go in. Instead, he entered the adjacent barn and climbed a ladder to the loft. Somehow, he managed to staunch the bleeding, and he waited.

Early the next morning, the girl came out of her house and walked into the barn. She followed the bloodstains up the ladder and nearly fainted when she saw her wounded friend. Verute brought him food, dressed his wounds, and gave him clean clothes. She then recommended that he leave, because her brother-in-law was a collaborator. That evening he left and hid in a wheat field. Luckily, the tall crop had not yet been harvested, and he was not discovered.

The days were very hot, and the nights were cold. Whenever she could, Verute brought him supplies. One day, she even brought him a note from his mother, who was still alive, as were most of his relatives. However, the Lithuanians had murdered his father.

A devout Catholic, Verute eventually told her local priest about everything that she had done for Motke. He suggested that she tell Motke to come to the church. Motke refused the offer and left that very evening. He traveled at night and hid during the day along the main road leading to Dvinsk, without food, water, or shelter. Finally, after much suffering and with considerable exertion, he reached the Dvina River a few weeks later. The ghetto was located on the river's southern shore.

He was captured by German soldiers, who thought he was a Russian spy or a partisan, and brought him to the citadel to be interrogated. The interrogations lasted for several days, and then the German soldiers transferred him to the ghetto's Latvian commander, who locked Motke in the hut. I found him the next day.

After he finished eating and telling us his sad but gripping story, I brought him to the ghetto's hospital, which was still (just barely) operating. They removed the shrapnel from his body and treated his injuries. Meanwhile, I told Shayke about my cousin, and several days after Motke was released from the hospital, Shayke came to visit and brought him several cooked potatoes. Those potatoes were very precious because Shayke was not working. His job at the post office had ended.

From the time I started working at the Ortskommandantur, I felt more secure, because I possessed a work permit, which stated that I was helping the German Army. The ghetto still contained many thousands of unemployed Jews, whose lives, as well as the lives of their family members, were in danger. In addition, there were many cases where the head of the family possessed the coveted schein, but their wives and children did not. The opposite was also true: many women worked while their husbands and children remained in the ghetto.

In my case, I received enough food at work for my own needs and was also able to help my cousin, who was slowly recovering.

Yet, I was worried about him, Shayke, Ben-Tzion Kutzin, and David Wechsler from Ponevezh, whom I had met in prison, as well as many other acquaintances, including a cousin of my friend, Yitzchak Weinerman, from Utian. None of them had the new schein, which now served as the sole document for Jewish workers from the ghetto.

On November 15, a crew suddenly and hastily began to build a wooden wall across the width of the ghetto. All the Jews in the ghetto sensed that this signified mortal danger. Everyone was visibly distressed because they did not know how to escape the looming threat. Their frightened eyes wondered who could help us now. It was clear that the murderers would use the wall as a way to separate those who were to be put to death from those who were to be kept alive.

And, in fact, following an extremely nerve-wracking day on Thursday, November 6, the terrible blow fell. Friday, November 7, the day of the Bolshevik Revolution, was the first day of the aktions, which had been carefully orchestrated by the SD and their Latvian collaborators. The aktions lasted for three consecutive days. Reinforcements were sent from Riga to help the local murderers.

As we heard from the Jews who hid throughout the ghetto and were eyewitnesses to the aktions, the Latvian guards were drunk and acted with unspeakable brutality. They searched everywhere, and when they found someone, they shot him on the spot.

Over the course of the three days, over eleven thousand innocent people perished.

On Friday, I went to work, as on every other day, even though the aktion had already begun. Early Saturday morning, loud orders forced every Jew in the ghetto, except for those in the hospital, into the courtyard. Whoever had a new work permit was ordered, together with the members of their work group, to climb the hill facing the entrance gate and wait for further orders from the SD.

As we had suspected, the fate of those remaining below had already been sealed. But we had assumed that the workers' family members were still protected. We waited outside in the cold and watched the events down below. The guards' shouts and blows reverberated through the air, as did their victims' moans and heartbreaking cries.

Our group was suddenly ordered to descend to the entrance gate for selection. We showed our papers. A Latvian guard approached one of the men in our group, a barber named Razz, whom he apparently recognized. Shouting and cursing, the guard beat him and then sent him to join those who were being put to death. The rest of us were allowed to go to work.

A somber mood prevailed that day. We could not stop thinking about those whose fate had been sealed when they were sent to the left and about those whom we still hoped to find among the living. When we returned to the ghetto that evening, we discovered that even the wives and children of the men in our group had been put to death. Tearfully and with bags of food in our hands, we entered the room where Tuviah's wife and their two small children were supposed to be waiting for us. But they were not there. Tuviah burst out crying, bitterly and loudly. When he finally calmed down somewhat, a few difficult minutes later, I had no words to comfort him.

On Sunday, the third day of the horrific actions, which, according to eyewitnesses, were extraordinarily vicious, we left for work as usual, at 7:00. No one spoke as we walked. We were in shock. It was cold and rainy. The German major ordered me to sweep the street and the courtyard in front of the Ortskommandantur. In the afternoon, after I had finished working outside, I was told to help Tuviah paint signs. I did not recognize the man who normally had a sense of humor and was filled with joie de vivre. He could not accept the fact that from now on, he was without a family and that no one needed him to bring them food. We returned to the ghetto, and I immediately ran to find my cousin Mordechai, my friend Shayke, and my other Lithuanian acquaintances, such as Ben-Tzion Kutzin and David Wechsler, who did not have work.

As it turned out, during the three days of the aktions, they all had hid in an attic under a pile of metal scraps, except for Mordechai, who spent the first two days hiding in a remote, dark corner of the attic. Then, on the third day, early in the morning, he and seven other people emerged from their hiding places and had no choice but to go into a public latrine, which was filled with sewage. They spent four hours immersed up to their necks. The men supported one short woman, lest she drown in the sewage.

Fortunately, although the Latvian guards and the SD men combed every single corner as they searched for hidden Jews, they did not find my cousin and the others.

After the searches had ended, they came out of the latrine. Somehow, after washing up, they managed to find clean clothes and shoes, and each one returned to where he had been before the aktions. That evening, I met my cousin Mordechai (Motke) after his "immersion." He still reeked of sewage. I thought: Man's innate will to live is so strong. It drives him to bold actions like these, even though life in the ghetto was unbearable!

Several days after the aktions, we heard that Ben-Tzion Kutzin from Ponevezh and Shmulke Peletz from Yanova had managed to escape to the town of Breslav. Earlier, there had been rumors that the Germans had slaughtered all the Jews in the White Russian towns on the Latvian border, but for some reason, they skipped over Breslav.

Personally, I did not plan on escaping, because I felt that it was difficult to outrun fate.

Motke, Shayke, my new friend and bunkmate Berke Kaplan, and several other young men were selected for construction work in the German military camp in the *Krepost*, the citadel on the other side of the Dvina River, facing the ghetto. I did not stay in the ghetto, either. At that time, my entire work group was transferred to barracks in a relatively large house on Tchetokshena Street in the center of town. This happened in the middle of November 1941.

I temporarily lost contact with my close friends. We each worked in separate places, and we did not meet again for another half a year until after that bitter, tragic day, May 1, the day of the ghetto's final liquidation.

On Sundays, I often had a chance to visit my few remaining acquaintances in the ghetto. They all feared that their end was near, but nevertheless, they retained a thin shred of hope that perhaps a miracle would happen and they would remain alive. According to the conversations I had with some of them, they were willing to endure the tremendous suffering that was their lot during the bitterly cold winter of 1942—including daily hunger—as long as they were not killed. I imagine that it was very difficult for them to subsist on the sparse rations that the ghetto authorities allotted them. Only a few of them had anything left to barter with the non-Jews in the city in exchange for food. I could not act as a go-between for them because I did not know any of the city's non-Jewish residents.

One time, in the spring, I managed to trade some clothes that I had received from a Jew in the ghetto for a loaf of bread and something else, which I do not remember. Tuviah had helped me perform the trade one evening. But then all of a sudden, there was a closure, and we were not allowed to enter the ghetto. To my great dismay and disappointment, I was unable to bring the supplies to the starving Jew in time, because like his fellow sufferers, he no longer needed food.

From the time we moved to the city through May 1942, I worked as a carpenter in the citadel, where they manufactured beds for the German Army. I worked together with a Jew named Yaakov Megrem, who was in his forties. The work was not overly difficult. We served as a support team to Austrian soldiers, who did the professional work of manufacturing the beds.

These soldiers treated us decently. We brought them the raw materials and then carried the finished products to the warehouses. In addition, we cleaned the workplace. They even allowed me to build myself a small cupboard to store my food. Our supervisors provided us with food rations, but we had to do the cooking ourselves. We used a relatively large kitchen for the cooking. Our group included several young women, who lived in a separate room, and they were the cooks. Every evening, when we returned from work, we each received a hot meal.

The major made sure that we all had suitable jobs, including producing signs. Only two men produced the signs, Tuviah Luvy and Moshe Ayerov, whom I mentioned previously.

One day, several of us were ordered to dig a pit outside the city, but we did not know why. However, as we rode back in a truck, we passed an open truck traveling toward the pit we had dug. A bound young man stood inside the truck. His facial features identified him as Russian. And then we understood. Apparently, the man had fought as a partisan against the German Army.

It was a harsh winter, but our apartment was heated, thanks to the major, who supplied us with kindling such as wood and coal. Curiously, nearly every evening, a young German soldier would visit us. Light haired and tall, he had an athlete's physique. As we understood it, his job was to keep track of what was going on in our living quarters. He would talk with us and entertain us with his skillful magic tricks. I remember that he showed us how to use one's teeth to lift a man by his belt. Since I was the youngest in our group, he picked me to demonstrate his method, and I actually managed to do the trick.

In order to lift our spirits, we would sometime organize dances for ourselves. Of course, we did this only when the soldier was not with us. Our group included an outstanding musician from Dvinsk, named Shimon Lefkovitz, who had conducted an orchestra in the city before the Soviets arrived. Somehow, he managed to obtain a mandolin in good condition and in our free time, after work, he would play it. I had learned to play the instrument when I was fourteen and was fairly proficient. Thus, when we danced, we would take turns playing.

One time, we obtained a bottle of vodka, and that evening, before our meal, we proposed a toast to our imminent liberation, which we really wanted to believe would come soon. After we drank, each person reacted differently. Most of us became more alert and joyful. But the liquor had the opposite effect on one man.

The man who had an unexpected reaction to the vodka was my friend, Tuviah Luvy. Suddenly, he burst into bitter tears, and as he was crying, he uttered a sentence that I still remember as I write these lines, "What am I trying to be happy about? That they killed my wife and my two children?"

I read in the German and Latvian newspapers that there was heavy fighting near Moscow and Leningrad in spite of the harsh winter. Based on the number of ambulances, which drove by on the citadel's main road where I worked, on their way to the military hospital, I realized that the German Army was no longer meandering through the Soviet Union. "General Winter" was now working against them. We hoped that they were in for a rerun of Napoleon Bonaparte's lesson at the gates of Moscow.

In February 1942, apparently in response to the increased demand for additional soldiers on the eastern front, all the Austrian soldiers who worked with me producing beds for the German Army were drafted on the same day. They were sent to the Tikhvin region, near Leningrad, where there were fierce battles, and civilian workers under the command of a German soldier replaced them. As I noted above, Yaakov Megrem and I would transfer the completed beds to the warehouse and clean the work area. Now, I was also forced to operate the woodcutting machine.

Once, as a result of my inexperience, I had a minor work accident. As I was pulling the wooden boards out of the machine, one of the fingers on my right hand got caught in the machine. I quickly ran to the nearby military first-aid station for treatment. They cleaned and bandaged my injured finger, and I returned to work.

Slowly, we adjusted to our daily routine during that winter. In order to survive, our thoughts and hopes were focused on the future, which was, in spite of the encouraging news from the fronts, rather hazy.

And then spring came. Nature came back to life, but the Nazis decided to direct their anger and frustrations, which stemmed from their failures on the battlefield, at the Jews of the ghetto. In spite of the cold, the hunger, and the diseases, approximately one thousand men and women, including the elderly and small children, were still alive in the ghetto.

As was the case during the previous aktions on November 6-7, the murderers once again chose May 1, International Workers' Day, to liquidate the ghetto. Only a few survived the ghetto's final aktion, and these survivors served as eyewitnesses to that which transpired in the ghetto's courtyard.

One of them, a seventeen year old named Yankele Sreisky, from the Lithuanian town of Shauliai, who was later to become my good friend, watched everything from his hiding place through a crack in the ghetto wall. He himself documented what he saw in his journal—a shocking story. This time, the murderers decided to kill everyone in the ghetto, including the Jewish policemen and the Kommitet, led by Misha Movshenzon and his wife Grunya. Whoever was not murdered in the ghetto was brought by truck to the Pogulyanka Forest where they were shot.

Thus ends the tragic chapter of the large and glorious Jewish population of Dvinsk and the surrounding area, including the Jewish refugees from Lithuania and even a number from Poland. Outside the ghetto, some four hundred men and women, including several teenagers and Shneur and Nechamah Eltzofen's four-year-old son, Michah'le, remained in several locations in the city and the citadel. They were left alive for the time being to serve the German Army.

As for me, I continued to live in the city on Tchetokshena Street (in the citadel), together with a handful of friends who also still worked at the German Ortskommandantur.

CHAPTER FOUR:

The Dvinsk Fortress

On May 5, 1942, my overseers at the Ortskommandantur in Dvinsk sent me to live and work in the fortress on the northwestern shore of the Dvina River, located approximately three kilometers from the center of town. I was assigned to the Wehrmacht's Construction and Renovation Unit, which was commanded by the *Oberzahlmeister* (Paymaster). The unit was known as *Heeresbaudienststelle* No. 100.

Although I preferred to work as a sign painter, I was assigned work as a house painter because they lacked professionals in this field. My living quarters were on the ground floor of a two-story house in the center of the fortress. German airmen lived above us; we shared a common entrance to the building.

I shared my quarters with a number of my fellow sufferers, my Jewish brothers, many of whom I knew from prison and from the ghetto. They had arrived here several months earlier. In particular, I was happy to find my cousin Motke Kuretsky; Shayke Eivensky, whom I had met in prison and who appears in the previous chapters; David Wechsler, the violin teacher from Ponevezh who was in his thirties; Moshe Ayerov, the biology student from

Mariampol; Avraham Orlovik from Kupishok; and many other Jews from Lithuania and from Dvinsk and its environs.

We all worked to the best of our abilities, renovating buildings in the fortress and in Dvinsk. Our overseers gave us food rations, which were more or less adequate, especially in contrast to the starvation rations we had received in the ghetto. Nevertheless, each man tried, as best as he could, to increase and vary his daily menu. We adopted the word *organiziren* (to organize) from the German soldiers. In practice, each person interpreted this concept according to his own imagination and talents.

Frequently, we worked near civilian workers, including Poles, Russians, and Latvians, who agreed to barter with us. In exchange for articles of clothing, we received food, including bread, butter, lard, and more. I had nothing of real value to exchange, so I used my drawing skills to obtain food.

At work, I met German soldiers who would order portraits of their families from me; in return, they would give me, depending on their generosity, half a loaf of army bread, butter, or other foodstuffs. Sometimes, they paid me with money, which I used to purchase essential items such as butter or pork from my roommate, Potash Yosef, a Dvinsk Jew in his forties. Before the war, I had abstained from eating pork, like most of the Jews in Utian, but under our current hostile circumstances, I could not resist the temptation.

Yossel had a unique sense of humor. He had his own language, which he learned in jail from professional thieves. Often he would use these special words to amuse us on the sad and difficult days that were our lot. For example, food was called *pichlovka* or *yushnik*; a policeman or soldier was a *manta*; and herring was *a schvimmer*. A brave and resourceful man, he used his connections with the city's non-Jewish residents to obtain good food, which he brought into the building with the help of various schemes. Obviously, not everyone had money to purchase these foodstuffs from him, but the very fact that the food was available greatly encouraged us all.

On Sundays, when we did not work, we tried to pass the time with music and entertainment. As I noted above, one of the men was David Wechsler, a music teacher who had brought his violin with him from the ghetto. Every day, after he returned from the city where he worked as a barber, he demonstrated his considerable talent and warmed our hearts with beautiful pieces of classical music. On Sundays, Moshe Ayerov, who was very talented at impersonations and recitations, would join him, and I would play on my mandolin, which I had brought from the city.

In addition, we would reminisce fondly about the old days before the war. We tried to make ourselves forget what lay ahead. It was as if we were saying to ourselves, "Let's live life today to the fullest extent possible, and let's not ruin our moods with thoughts about the future!"

We believed that as long as the Germans needed us to work, we were more or less protected. They were concerned about our personal hygiene, and every once in a while, we were taken to a bathhouse in the city. We had a small kitchenette, and we could use it to cook or fry. Every day, two women, Sorah Megrem and

Rucheleh, whose last name I do not remember, made soup for us from the rations we received from the Germans.

The fortress where we lived and worked from May 1942 to October 1943 had been built by the czars and had been controlled by the Russians for most of its history. In 1918 the Latvians assumed control of the fortress after they gained independence, but then the Soviets seized it when they invaded Latvia in June 1940. During the Soviet retreat, there had been no time to destroy the fortress or its warehouses filled with ammunition, clothing, and food; it all fell like ripe fruit into the hands of the German Army.

The fortress covered several square kilometers, had four gates, and included many different types of buildings: barracks, stables, warehouses, hospitals, workshops, and even a church. Giant walls and dry moats encircled the fortress, and it was crisscrossed by a number of roads. In addition, it contained several newer three-story structures as well as a public park in the center. Every day, we could hear marching songs coming from the park, which was where the various companies of German soldiers would drill.

During the year or so that I painted rooms in Dvinsk for the Wehrmacht soldiers, I would place myself at risk and buy newspapers—mostly in German but sometimes in Latvian—at kiosks. Thus, I learned that along the entire front, the Germans had advanced during 1942 deep into giant Russia, and they now stood at the gates of Moscow and Leningrad. In addition, they had conquered all of Ukraine, had reached the outskirts of Stalingrad on the banks of the Volga River, and were advancing toward the oil fields in the Caucasus.

We knew that we were the only ones left of the sixteen thousand Jews who had lived in the ghetto when it was first established. At this point, approximately two hundred fifty men and women lived in the fortress, and about another one hundred eighty Jews lived and worked for the Wehrmacht in Dvinsk itself. We kept in touch with the latter on Sundays when they would come visit us.

We worked for three military units in the fortress. As I noted above, Construction and Renovation Unit No. 100, where we lived and worked, employed some fifty men. Four young men worked in the stables, which belonged to Unit No. 200, and about two hundred Jews, mostly women, worked for Unit No. 322, in sewing workshops and warehouses. In addition, two young children, who were cared for by their parents, and two teenagers, who had been adopted by some of the adults, lived with us as well.

Those who worked for Unit No. 322 lived in a two-story house, which was located not too far from us. The Jews lived on the second floor, and Russian prisoners of war, who performed assorted jobs for the Wehrmacht, lived on the first floor. There were bars on their windows, but they would chat with the Jewish women and girls through the bars. The women and some of the Jewish men who worked in the sewing workshops and the warehouses mended and cleaned military uniforms. They were overseen by German soldiers.

In spite of the constant surveillance, these Jewish women managed to take various articles of clothing from the warehouses. The clothes were eventually sold to non-Jewish civilians in exchange for food. But then one day, a woman was caught in the city without her yellow star, and she was found to be carrying a sealskin vest. The woman was sent to prison, where she was shot dead. After this incident, the Unit No. 322 workers' conditions changed for the worse.

During my time in the fortress, there were two other cases when Jews lost their lives. First, a Dvinsk Jew named Bormat, who was about sixty years old, was caught in the city's marketplace without a yellow star. He was thrown in prison where he was shot for his "terrible crime." And then, Eli Kurland, a young Jew in his thirties, who was also from Dvinsk and who worked as a tinsmith for our unit, was imprisoned and executed in a case of mistaken identity. He was confused with another Jew with the same last name, who had been active during the Soviet era. Except for these two instances, no one else was put to death during my stay in the fortress.

Following the German defeat in Stalingrad and their retreat from wide swaths of Russian and Ukrainian territory in the spring of 1943, we noticed that the German soldiers and officers who worked with us were becoming sadder by the day. We tried not to act happy in front of them. Yet, in our hearts, we felt that not all was lost if the Red Army was driving the Germans back. But what would happen to us?

In the spring of 1943, I became very close to a pretty, twenty-one-year-old girl named Shayna'le Ichilov from Dvinsk. She lived in the building that housed the Unit No. 322 workers and worked in that unit's military sewing workshop. Out of her entire extended family, only her father Shalom was left. He was a goodhearted, gentle man in his fifties, and I was very fond of him. He lived and worked in the city and he always found us together when he visited his daughter on Sundays.

Shortly before the war, Shayna'le had married a young man her age, named Chaim, whom I had met in prison in July 1941. He was a nice, good-looking man. During one of the aktions in the Dvinsk Ghetto, he was put to death, together with thousands of other victims, in the Pogulyanka Forest.

When Shayna'le and I met, I could still see the sadness in her blue eyes, as she mourned her husband and most of her relatives. I would visit her every evening and especially on Sundays. We discovered that we had much in common, including a love of writing poetry and music. I found her to be dedicated, frank, and faithful. What more could one ask of another?

Once, while I was visiting Shayna'le on a summer evening in 1943, she told me that she had begun to write Yiddish songs about our lives in the Dvinsk Ghetto and our current lives in the fortress. She put her lyrics to popular Russian songs. Obviously, I was very happy about her accomplishment because I understood that by writing songs about such painful subjects, she was freeing herself from painful emotional baggage. I also wrote several poems during that time about our difficult lives, but I did not look for appropriate music for my lyrics.

Hoping that someone would organize an evening of music and entertainment, we started to rehearse. Shayna'le would sing her songs, and I would accompany her on my mandolin. And indeed a

Jew whose name escapes me organized such an evening for the Unit No. 322 workers. On one Saturday night, we got together to express whatever interested us and touched our hearts. It was a very emotional evening. A young woman named Chaya'le Epstein sang Yiddish and Russian songs, and Yehuda Monitz, a man in his late twenties who had a beautiful voice, sang some songs in Russian. I still remember one of these songs. It was called "*Ulitza*" ("The Street"). I read a few of my poems, which focused on our daily lives and brought several members of the audience to tears. And of course, I accompanied Shayna'le with my mandolin as she sang.

One day, during one of my regular visits, Shayna'le was very upset. She had lost her engagement ring in the shower. I realized that the ring was very precious to her, over and above its material value because it was all she had left, besides her memories, from her previous life and her late husband. I went down to the showers and found the ring in a drainpipe. Another time, she surprised me with a pair of winter pants, which she had sewn out of good quality cloth while working in the military sewing workshop. She gave me the present just in time, because autumn was approaching. It was very rainy and cold outside.

Shayna'le was very pretty, but I fell in love with her personality. When we would talk and share our inner thoughts, she was soft-spoken, courteous, and a great listener. In the evenings, we loved to sit in her tiny room, which held two beds (her roommate worked with her in the sewing workshop), and to fantasize about the unknown future. We both hoped to be liberated from our bleak reality to build a life together, and to live, in accordance with her wishes, in Dvinsk. She would frequently say, "Apparently, fate wants me to continue my life with a different Chaim, instead of the Chaim who perished."

My cousin Motke and my friend Shayke found their destinies with two sisters from the Gutterman family of Dvinsk. They lived in the fortress with their mother, their older sister Ella, whose husband was murdered in the Dvinsk Ghetto, and their younger brother Laizer'l, who was about fourteen. Motke's girlfriend was named Hinda, who was about eighteen years old. Shayke's girlfriend was named Golda, and she was two years younger than Hinda. They were a very warm and cohesive family.

The three sisters worked in the military laundry, which was very difficult work. The mother kept house for the family, and Laizer'l worked in the military kitchen. The sisters' overseer in the laundry provided them with essential goods, and Shayke, Motke, and Laizer'l took care of the rest.

As far as the mother was concerned, Motke and Shayke were part of the family, and she called them, *kinder* (children). They once admitted to me that they were deeply in love with Hinda and Golda and felt very welcome within their family. My cousin and my friend worked together painting rooms for the army. They spent the evenings with their girlfriends and returned to their room in our building only to sleep. Apparently, time and nature did their thing, and these and other similar relationships developed all the time in the fortress between young Jewish men and women.

As I noted above, I knew what was happening on the fronts from the German and Latvian newspapers. However, I knew very little about what was happening to European Jewry. The only thing I knew was that nearly all of Lithuanian and Latvian Jewry had perished.

In April 1943, I learned about the Warsaw Ghetto uprising and of the existence of death camps in Poland. These camps were designed for the physical annihilation of European Jewry, using gas chambers and crematoria. From the same sources, I also learned of the existence of ghettos in Vilna, Kovno, and Shavliai where the remnant of Lithuanian Jewry had been concentrated.

That summer, a supply unit from Lithuania passed by the fortress. They were on their way back from the Russian front to the northeast of Latvia. When we heard about the unit, several of us from Lithuania went out to meet them to learn more about what had happened to Lithuanian Jewry. The soldiers were standing next to their wagons, which were harnessed to their horses. They were surprised to see living Lithuanian Jews who spoke their language. According to the soldiers, they came from towns in northern Lithuania, including my hometown of Utian. They confirmed that there were no living Jews in the entire region.

One of them was from Utian, and I recognized him as a simple laborer who had worked in Dov Sher's bakery. (Dov Sher was one of Utian's most prominent citizens.) The Lithuanian soldier told me in great detail about how the Jews of Utian were shot to death in the Rashe Forest, about three or four kilometers northwest of Utian. Based on his exact description of the massacre, I realized that he was one of the depraved murderers. He said that he was recently drafted by the German Army to support their soldiers on the front. Before we said goodbye, they gave us bread and other foodstuffs, including butter and smoked ham.

As the front drew closer to Dvinsk, we became increasingly concerned. There was a strong possibility that if they would have to retreat from Dvinsk, the Germans would not leave us behind. Either they would transfer us elsewhere or they would execute us.

Thus, during the summer of 1943, there were several failed escape attempts. One such attempt occurred in May of that year. A young man named Gutke Yachnin, who worked, together with three other young Jewish men, as a wagon driver in the Unit No. 200 stables, decided to escape from the fortress with some Russian prisoners. Unfortunately, the prisoners simply took advantage of his knowledge of the immediate area, stole his pistol and essential goods, and deserted him. Luckily, however, he managed to make it back to work after a two-day absence, without being discovered.

Subsequently, there were two other similar failed attempts. In the first case, three girls, who were about sixteen or seventeen and worked together for Unit No. 322, arranged an escape with three prisoners of war. Several days later, the girls returned to their unit because, as in the previous incident, the prisoners had taken advantage of the girls' help and then deserted them. Eventually, the girls were thrown in prison and executed.

In the second case, according to what we heard, four men and two women set out to the east of Dvinsk to find the partisans' base, together with a German who agreed to take them to the forest in exchange for payment. However, the German threw them out of his vehicle shortly after they left. Some of the Jews continued on to the forest where they were soon captured. The others returned to the fortress; fortunately, the Germans never discovered that they had been missing.

Following these two incidents, the Germans treated us even more harshly. In particular, the Jews who worked for Unit No. 322 received a severe warning from the unit's commanders. In order to prevent the Jews from escaping from the fortress, the Germans erected a brick wall, which was about 2.5-3 meters high, between two adjacent buildings. The Unit No. 322 workers lived in one building, and the second building housed the army's German civilian employees. Glass shards, which were cemented into the top of the wall, served as further deterrence against any escape attempts.

One of my friends in Unit No. 100, David Blayer, a seventeen year old from Dvinsk, worked for the *Gebietskommissar* (Dvinsk's district commissioner) and had access to a radio. He would tell me about the situation on the fronts. According to what he had heard, the front was rapidly approaching Dvinsk. In addition, he informed me that he had acquired a pistol with bullets and that he did not intend to give up his young life cheaply to the Germans.

Other Jewish teenagers in the fortress also managed to acquire weapons and planned on escaping to the partisan camps in the White Russian forests. If they did not reach their destinations, they would at least be able to use the weapons, if necessary, against our murderous enemies.

One such teenager was particularly brave. His name was Chaim'ke Gordon, and he had managed to acquire a pistol and many bullets via all sorts of daring schemes. These young people did not try to hide their secrets from us. But even if one had enough money to purchase a weapon, one still needed to find the right man to handle the transaction.

I realized that I did not have enough money to buy a gun, and many other young people, including Yankele Sreisky from Lithuania, were in the same boat. I would meet with Yankele, who worked as a tailor for Unit No. 322, in the evenings after work, and we would discuss our situation. Both of us were aware of the fact that, under the circumstances, we had to be prepared for passive resistance in case of emergency.

In September 1943, we learned that Shayke, my cousin Motke, and Berke Kaplan had disappeared. That day, a Friday, Motke had come to my room after work, holding his work overalls, which had been painted in camouflage colors and wrapped in heavy paper. He asked if he could leave it in my room. His face was tense. I agreed because I had recently been camouflaging the fortress's roofs. Thus, if the package were found, the Germans would not be suspicious. And indeed, the next day, the Germans came and discovered the package but left without asking any questions. I was very surprised that Shayke and Berke had not told me that they intended to escape. Nevertheless I prayed for their success.

Shortly thereafter, we heard rumors that the three had reached a partisan camp in White Russia. Unfortunately, Berke Kaplan was killed in a battle against the Germans who had attacked their base.

I read in the German papers that during the recent battles, the German Army was continuously retreating along the entire eastern front. We realized that the moment of truth was arriving, and we were very concerned. On October 27, we heard that the Germans were planning to transfer us from the fortress to another location. A group of young people, including Yankele Sreisky and me, decided to post a guard in our building and to change shifts every four hours. I went first. Meanwhile, the others lay down in their clothes to rest or sleep. When I finished my shift, Yankele Sreisky came to take over.

At about 3:00 or 4:00 a.m., when a tense stillness prevailed, Yankele suddenly shouted in Yiddish, *"Men iz gekumen unz nemen!"* ("They've come to get us!") He repeated his warning several times. The Latvian guards, who were quite skilled at murdering Jews, burst into our building's courtyard with loud shouts. Several shots were heard; everyone panicked. We started to run in every direction, like blind mice.

I ran down from the second floor to the wall separating our building from the adjacent courtyard. As I noted above, the wall was topped with sharp glass shards, which were attached with hard cement. On my first attempt, I managed to leap over the wall! My hands were dripping blood, but I paid no attention.

It was pitch black as I searched for a hiding place in the courtyard where every morning I would report to my elderly German overseer. We would gather our tools and painting materials here and then head to work in the fortress. The overseer was a surly, bad-tempered man, and I did not dare to wake him to ask for his help. He lived on the ground floor of a two-story building.

After a brief search, I decided to hide in an empty paint barrel, which I turned upside down on top of myself. I sat inside bent over and tense as I awaited further developments. A Latvian guard soon discovered me, when he kicked the barrel that had become my temporary home. He ordered me to accompany him. We went to our building's courtyard where all the Jewish residents were lined up in threes. I joined a row.

Looking around, I saw Shayna'le and her father, who had been brought to the fortress with all the other Jews who worked in the city. We exchanged glances without saying a word. Our eyes said it all. The end was near.

Some of the guards watched us, and the others searched for the Jews who were hiding. Every so often, a new group of Jews joined our rows after the guards had discovered them. We were forced to remain standing in the cold for a long time as the tension continued to grow. It started to rain and the guards ordered us forward. We left the courtyard and headed toward the exit gate, which led to the city. Not far from the gate, Yehuda Monitz, whom I mentioned previously, broke out of line and began running toward one of the courtyards. Immediately, some German soldiers, who happened to see him running, gave chase. Within a few seconds, shots rang out. That wonderful, precious, young man was dead.

As we marched, I noticed that my acquaintance Efraim Kobb, who worked in the fortress with a Jew named Chaim (I do not remember his last name), was one row ahead of me. It turned out that Chaim had tried to kill himself by drinking strong alcohol when the Latvian guards entered the fortress. However, he succeeded only in getting very drunk. Efraim supported him as they marched.

We arrived at the freight train station, which was located near the park behind the prison where those same Latvian murderers had shot hundreds of our Jewish brothers on July 9, 1941. As we stood, silent and anxious, next to the railway tracks, the rain continued throughout the day until the evening. The gloomy sky mirrored our spirits. We wondered why the Latvian murderers had decided to take us by freight train to be killed when they could have accomplished the same thing several kilometers away in the Pogulyanka Forest.

Could it be that there would be a different ending this time? Maybe the Germans still needed our services for their war effort? Maybe.

When evening fell and everyone was hungry, drenched, and shivering from the cold, we were forced into the freight cars. There were bars on the windows, and as we crowded together, we were miserably aware of the fact that we had no place to run. We were all immersed in our own thoughts and hopes. Some of us were busy plotting daring schemes to escape the unknown by jumping out of the window, once the train would start moving.

One thing was clear: We were traveling westward. The train began to move, slowly at first, and then gradually it picked up speed.

Thus ends another chapter of forced labor and uncertainty, which lasted nearly a year and a half in the Dvinsk Fortress.

CHAPTER FIVE:

Riga – The Kaiserwald Concentration Camp and the Spilve Labor Camp

Arrival in Riga

On the morning of October 30, 1943, a cold, pre-winter day, we—the approximately three hundred Jews who, thanks to great and supernatural miracles, had survived Dvinsk's ghetto, fortress, and prison during the time of the Nazi's savage massacres—arrived in the Skirotava train station, outside Riga.

Packed into filthy, unheated freight train cars, we had spent the entire night traveling from Dvinsk to Riga, without food, drink, or any way to relieve ourselves. Lying on the cold, hard floor, we feared for our lives. When the armed guards, the Germans and Latvians who had accompanied us on the entire journey, ordered us to exit the cars quickly, we were finally able to breathe sighs of relief.

For the next few hours, we were allowed to wander around freely. We began searching for our relatives, friends, and any Jewish brethren whom we had met during our incarceration in the Dvinsk Fortress. Fortune smiled on me. I suddenly bumped into my best friend from that period, Baruch Kwill from Kraslava.

Baruch told me that, panicked and frightened, he and several other Jews had run in every direction in search of a hiding place from their pursuers. However, they were eventually found by the Nazis, who brought them to the courtyard where the rows of Jews stood and awaited their unknown fate.

We also learned of our esteemed friends' tragic end. On that night of October 29, the Latvian police surrounded the two-story house, where we had lived together with the Soviet prisoners, and headed to the attic in search of Jews. It was there that David Wechsler, the music teacher from Ponevezh, Lithuania, and Simanovitch, the watchmaker from Dvinsk, were found and shot to death.

In addition, several Jews committed suicide out of desperation. Moshe Techer poisoned himself, and Epskin hung himself. Avraham Orlovik from Kupishok, Lithuania, broke his legs while jumping off the fortress's wall. Ben-Tzion Katz shot his mother to death with the pistol he had acquired earlier, and a husband shot his wife and young son to death. His name was Ben-Tzion Sheffer. We all believed that we were about to be massacred, and these people acted out of sheer hopelessness and despair.

We also heard that a Jew had jumped out of a window from the moving train, and someone else had swallowed poison.

Suddenly, trucks arrived, and we were transported to the Riga Ghetto, which had been emptied of its Jewish prisoners, who had all been executed. After our names were written down, we were taken to a large concentration camp, which was run by the SS. The camp, which was called Kaiserwald (The King's Forest), covered a huge tract of land. It contained a number of wooden structures arranged symmetrically along the camp's entire length and width. The commandant was a high-ranking SS officer, *Obersturmbannführer* (Lieutenant Colonel) Krause. Assorted nationals, mostly Poles with criminal pasts, supported the SS men who worked at headquarters, located at some distance from the rest of the camp.

Once again they counted us, and the men were separated from the women and children. Miraculously, several children had remained alive until they arrived at Kaiserwald.

We, the men, were led to a makeshift bathhouse and ordered to wash hastily in cold water and without soap. After the quick rinse, we were not allowed to touch our old clothes. Instead, we were supplied with different clothes, but we were permitted to reuse our original shoes.

Each man received a scrap of white cloth with a number, which was to be worn on the left side of one's shirt. Then we were informed that we no longer belonged to the *Wehrmacht* (the German Army) but were now the property of the SS. We were told that we must maintain discipline and obey all orders and commands.

Thus, we stood outside throughout that autumn day, suffering from both cold and hunger. Mercifully, it was not raining. In the evening, we were each given bread and a bit of margarine and taken to the shack. There were no beds, and we had to sleep that night on the cold floor.

Shalom Ichilov, the tailor from Dvinsk, lay next to me. His daughter Shayna'le and I had been friends for nearly two years. She was the only one he had left. The rest of their family had been killed in the aktions and massacres that the Nazis had perpetrated in Dvinsk's prison and ghetto.

The two of us were now greatly encouraged by our physical proximity. At 6:00 in the morning, we were awakened by a bell. There was no need to get dressed, because we had slept in our clothes. We were ordered outside and divided into labor companies. Each company was sent to a different job within the camp.

Together with a number of other young men my age, I was attached to the camp's *Innendienst* (internal service). That day, Moshe Ayerov, with much emotion, asked me if I would be willing to cooperate with him in terms of obtaining food and mutual assistance. Naturally, I agreed because friendship was very important to us, like air to breathe.

All day, we dragged boxes and crates filled with potatoes to the camp's kitchen. Contrary to the overseers' orders, we carried the crates near the women's shack. This allowed those hungry women, who had arrived with us from Dvinsk the day before, to grab a few potatoes. Somehow they then managed to cut the potatoes into small pieces and roast them over the small tin stoves, which were used to heat the shacks.

The SS female overseers would punish the women for "offenses" such as these and beat them viciously and pitilessly. Apparently, however, hunger overcomes the fear of punishment, and the starving women continued to take the potatoes.

One of these women was the aforementioned Shayna'le. We would exchange a few words. Mainly, I would give her regards from her father. She was glad that we were together. It lifted her spirits.

Appell (Roll call) was held twice a day, at 6:00 a.m. and at around 6:00 p.m., to count the prisoners (called *Haftlinge* in German) and to ensure that no one was missing.

Those of us who stayed behind for "internal service," as well as the weak and the sick, were not permitted to enter our shack until after the second roll call, which coincided with the end of work. The Jews from Riga, who had been brought to Kaiserwald before our arrival, secretly warned us to beware of the SS officers and their assistants. We were warned to remain vigilant at all times in order to avoid the SS men's ruthless beatings.

On Sunday, November 7, after a week in Kaiserwald, we were awakened for the early morning roll call, and the SS officers asked each one of us individually to state our professions and ages. At the end of the roll call, a number of trucks arrived and took most of the Jews who had come from Dvinsk to various labor camps in Riga and the surrounding area, including HKP, TVL, Dundagen, and Spilve. Some of the women from Dvinsk shared the same fate.

We were strictly forbidden to talk to each other, and as a result, I did not know what happened to my friends or where they were sent. By chance, I later learned that Baruch Kwill and an entire company of Jews were sent to Dundagen, where the conditions were brutal. Moshe Ayerov fared no better. He was sent to a labor camp in Estonia, which was run by SS men, who forced the prisoners to do hard labor.

When I was asked about my age and profession, I replied that I was twenty-two and that I worked as a sign maker. Based on my response, I was sent to work at the Riga Airport.

The Spilve Labor Camp

This camp, located in an area known as Slokas Iela, had been a beer factory before the war. It was situated several kilometers from the Riga Airport on the southern shore of the Dvina River.

Most of the Jews whom I met in Spilve came from the Kovno Ghetto. They numbered about one thousand men and women, including several children and even a few married couples. Before arriving in Spilve, these Kovno Jews had worked in the Aleksotas Airport on the outskirts of Kovno. In addition to the Kovno Jews, there were Latvian, German, Austrian, and Czech Jews, who had been brought here after the liquidation of the Riga Ghetto.

When I arrived at the camp, I discovered that the guards resembled the guards at Kaiserwald. The officers were all SS men, who treated the Jewish prisoners brutally.

These officers were led by the infamous Gustav Sorge, whose reputation for sadism and barbarism had spread to every ghetto and labor camp throughout occupied Europe. Known as *Der*

Eiserne Gustav (The Iron Gustav), he was a tall, slim man with a long, slender nose and watery eyes. A cruel smile constantly played on his thin lips.

Throughout the cold, rainy autumn and the freezing winter, this ruthless devil would step out of his office twice a day to receive the results of the roll calls. Dressed in a long, black coat and shiny, black boots, he would hold his whip in his hands. Speaking in a harsh monotone, he would warn us to obey every order and command. His appearance and voice instilled fear and terror in us. But at the same time, we felt disgust and loathing toward him. He would devise cruel and unusual—truly diabolical—means of tormenting those who dared to defy his sadistic, ironclad rules.

I remember one instance when a skinny, bespectacled Jew from Germany, who was about twenty years old, failed to obey a certain command. This happened during the morning roll call, before we left for work. Sorge, the Nazi commander, ordered the young man to step out of line, kneel, raise his hands, and stay that way without moving. I have no idea how long the poor Jew remained in this humiliating and degrading position because the rest of us were sent to work.

Two Jews were appointed by the SS to run the roll calls. They counted the men and women separately, ensured that no one was missing, and delivered the results to the camp's commanders. One of these Jewish overseers was Abba Tzapp, about thirty-four years old or even less. He had a strong build and was a former soccer player from Vilkomir, Lithuania. The second overseer, who was about the same age, was a German Jew named Metzger. They served the Germans on a daily basis. If someone was missing upon our return from work, they would force all of us to stand outside in the cold winter weather until they could determine the cause of the person's absence.

Every morning, a German Jew named Hekster was appointed by the Germans to send the workers off to their jobs. A tall, dignified, and intelligent man, he was about forty years old and wore glasses. Tzapp was in charge of distributing the clothes, shoes, and food. He lived in a private room, together with his wife, who oversaw the women, and their two young daughters, a thirteen year old and a four year old, under much better conditions than the rest of us. Their room was located on the second floor, where my workmates and I lived. Tzapp adored hard liquor. A number of Jews who worked outside of Spilve were able to obtain liquor for him, and as a result, they enjoyed greater privileges.

Only the Jews who worked for *Innendienst* ("internal service")— in the kitchen, the carpentry shop, the cobbler's workshop, or the clothing repair shop—remained in the camp. One of these Jews was a young barber from Kovno, who served the SS men. The Germans ordered him to use his scissors to make a special part in the middle of the Jews' heads, as a way of easily identifying them should they escape. We referred to this part as *Lausenstrasse* (Lice Road). The Jewish women were forced to have their heads completely shaved.

When I arrived in Spilve from Kaiserwald, I was placed in a company of fourteen Jews who worked at the Riga Airport. We worked for the German air force in different capacities. The sign makers, myself included, worked in the same room as the carpenters.

I worked with a Jew from Riga, who had miraculously survived the Nazi aktions in the Riga Ghetto. According to him, he was about fifty-three years old, but he looked as if he were seventy. He walked with a stoop and his hands shook. His last name was Meyeran, and he was the sole survivor of his entire family. He was addicted to alcohol, and when he was not drinking, he was unable to complete the assignments we were given by the German air force. Yet, the Germans were aware that he was an outstanding sign painter.

Our company was headed by a man named Alexanderovitch, a Pole who had come from Riga. In order to ensure that the assignments were completed, Alexanderovitch would regularly supply Meyeran with 90 percent alcohol. Meyeran would dilute the alcohol with some water and drink it with great pleasure. After he drank, his hands would stop shaking, and he would be able to do the work. With reddened cheeks, he would take a few bites of black bread. It was as if at that moment, he was the happiest man in the world.

A Jew from Padovicz, Czechoslovakia, named Troller, who was about fifty years old, also worked with us. A strong, heavyset man, he walked with a limp because he had been injured while fighting during World War I. He did not know Yiddish and spoke to us only in German. He was a skilled professional.

My job was to prepare the paint, which I received from the warehouse, managed by our chief foreman, a German civilian named Schmidt. He was from Prussia and had an engineering degree. In addition, I prepared the backgrounds upon which the signs were printed.

In that same one-story, wooden building, there were also a number of salaried Christians from Riga as well as several Jewish carpenters from our company—Plutkin, about fifty years old, from Riga; Levitt, about fifty, also from Riga; and Shaymeh Lumiansky, fifty-three, from Kovno.

Four locksmiths from our company worked in the adjacent building: Shapira and Wasserman from Riga, and Moshe Lupeikin and Melech from Kovno. All four men were in their thirties.

Several others worked in the same building. Kretchmer from Riga, who was about sixty, was a glazier, and Pruskauer from Czechoslovakia was an electrician. In addition, Wagenheim, who was about thirty, was a shoemaker, and Shimon Kagan, about sixty, was a tinsmith.

Schmidt, our foreman, treated us kindly and fairly. We received the same treatment from the armed guard, a German airman, who accompanied our company to and from work. They would talk to us and sometimes even make jokes to lift our spirits.

I was particularly friendly with Shaymeh Lumiansky from Lithuania. When I told him everything that had happened to me in Dvinsk and all that had transpired from the day we fled Utian, he realized that I had met his sister Baila, her husband, and their children. They had fled Yanova by foot, and on the train that was supposed to take us from Dvinsk to Riga, they were among the many Jewish refugees trying to escape the Nazis' claws. When that train stopped just outside of Dvinsk, Lumiansky's sister and her family joined the small band of Lithuanian Jews, including my mother—may Hashem avenge her blood—and me, who decided to remain together as long as the dangerous situation allowed.

During the first few days of the war, Lumiansky had lost his wife, his three daughters, and his only son on the road from Kovno to Latvia. He treated me like a son and talked about his family and his life before the war. He also told me about several things that had happened in Spilve before I arrived. For instance, he told me about Schumacher, a German butcher from Hamburg, who now served in Spilve. When he would distribute food to the Jewish workers, he would stand on a balcony and throw pieces of bread to the starving Jews. And as these unfortunates scampered to collect the bread, he would incite his wolf dogs and set them on the Jews. The dogs would attack and bite the Jews.

Staving off hunger

We were given what could best be described as starvation rations. As we used to say, "It's not enough to live on, but it's too much to die from." Thus, we all sought ways to increase and supplement our food allotments.

Each day at noon, we were served a vat filled with a hot brown-green liquid at work. In order to find a single pea, a lone grain of barley, or a sliver of potato, one needed a microscope. This soup was our lunch. The same vat was then carried to all the Jewish labor companies that were spread out over the huge airfield. Not only did the thin soup lack any calories, but sometimes it was not even hot enough.

Many of the labor companies in the airfield, especially the female ones but also some of the male companies, had no specific job. They worked very hard in every kind of weather. They dug ditches, transferred building supplies from place to place, and even loaded ammunition onto German fighter planes.

At Spilve, work began at 7:00 a.m. and continued until 6:00 p.m., with a short lunch break. The "lunch soup" arrived during this recess, and since there was nothing else, we eagerly looked forward to it.

At the end of the workday, each room received a 1-kilogram loaf of bread, which was to be divided among four men, and a tiny portion of margarine. To drink, we were given a pot of tea or coffee, which had been sweetened with a bit of sugar. In the morning before we left for work, we received the same drink.

I do not know how other people apportioned their loaf of bread, which was combined with wood shavings to increase its weight and volume. However, in our room, we tried to divide it equally, so that no one would feel deprived. It became a ritual of a sort: One man would cut the loaf into four pieces and then turn his back to the bread. A second man would then point at each piece and ask, "Whose?" and the first man would call out everyone's names.

Most of the men in my room on the second floor of the wide building belonged to our labor company. We were like a family and lived in friendship and brotherhood. We slept on wooden bunk beds with straw mattresses, straw pillows, and thin wool blankets.

In the winter, the two-story building was unheated. Thus, in spite of the crowded conditions, the rooms were bitterly cold. Nevertheless, notwithstanding the difficulties, we managed to maintain peace and quiet, more or less. Yet, we were all racked with hunger and asked ourselves, "What will happen to us in the coming days?"

During my stay in Spilve, I came up with a plan. First, I needed an extra set of work clothes or an overall, which did not have the patch with my personal number: 96086. This way, if the opportunity should present itself, I would be able to escape. Eventually, I obtained such an overall, and I hid it underneath my straw mattress.

Next, according to my plan, I needed to find a temporary hiding place at the home of a Latvian or Russian family. This was a very risky gamble, which had minimal chance of succeeding because, for the most part, the local Christian population was not exactly enamored with us, to put it mildly. But I had no other option. Deep down, I harbored a faint glimmer of hope that we would be liberated because every so often we heard dramatic news from the front, mainly from German or Latvian newspaper fragments.

We waged a never-ending war against the oppressive hunger and were jealous of satiated people. The crushing hunger was unbearable, but fortunately, we experienced an odd paradox. The more the SS persecuted us with hard labor, incessant suffering, hunger, and degradation just because we were Jewish, the more our spirits were lifted and the greater our desire to be liberated from Spilve's intolerable and inhuman conditions.

We were obsessed with food, which we had to obtain using various schemes in order to survive. At the carpentry shop in the airfield where I worked, the Christian workers would offer us food, such as bread, butter, eggs, and more, in exchange for valuables such as gold coins from the period of the Russian tsars and five or ten ruble coins. Due to their color, the latter were known as *chazairim'lach* (piglets) in Yiddish. In addition, the Christians asked us to get them gold rings, watches, and so on. But since none of the Jews in Spilve had such valuables—everything had been stolen from us long before—we could not accept the Christian carpenters' offer, and we continued to suffer from hunger.

Occasionally, I was able to obtain half a loaf of bread or other food by secretly removing bottles of expensive lacquer from our workroom and exchanging them with the local Christians. One of my roommates, a young man from Kovno, handled the trade. In return for his efforts, we split our profits.

I had to act quickly and carefully. First, I would find empty bottles and then fill them clandestinely from the large vat. Next, I would conceal the bottles in a dark, hidden corner. Each day, before leaving work, I would remove one bottle, place it inside the bottom half of my overall, and tie it tightly to my leg. Then, with fear and apprehension, I would walk past the guards and return to the camp.

For a long while, I continued to risk my life in this fashion. I discovered that hunger is stronger than man's will and nature and can bring him down to a degrading level.

As I did in the Dvinsk Fortress, I painted portraits from photographs for the German soldiers, who took advantage of my drawing skills. In exchange, they paid me with half a loaf of bread or sometimes even less. However, the soldiers were given bread of a different caliber.

Near the airfield, about two hundred meters from where I worked, there was a one-story house with a kitchen and dining room, where the German officers who served in the airport would eat three times a day. Every afternoon, between 1:00 and 2:00, a Russian boy, who seemed to be about fifteen years old, would arrive, driving a horse and wagon with a large, unclean barrel on top. The boy would collect any leftover food from the lunch plates and platters in the kitchen as well as the water used to wash the dishes. This mixture was used to feed the pigs that the German Army raised for food.

We devised various schemes to get our hands on this "treasure." For instance, we would stop working and creep over, one by one or in pairs, near the wagon. When we saw it leave the kitchen and dining room and head toward the barn, we would grab tin plates. And as the wagon turned from one alley into a second alley, we would quickly fill our dishes with the leftovers from the barrel. This happened nearly every day and went on for a long while. We had to eat the food immediately, because by the following day, the food would have spoiled and become inedible.

Sometimes I would bring a bowl of what we used to call "swine soup" to a hungry Jew, who was unable to obtain extra food, in order to provide some nourishment to his famished body.

Lumiansky, the Lithuanian Jew, once told me that in late 1942, before I arrived in Riga, a pot of rice porridge burned. Since the ruined porridge could not be served to the German officers, it was thrown into a deep pit. The snow, which fell continuously that winter, soon covered the pit. Due to the intense cold, the porridge froze and turned into a solid mass. When the freezing weather was over, the starving Jews who had worked near the buried "treasure" removed the frozen porridge from the pit and had a feast.

We had no choice but to try to obtain food by any means possible. Winter was particularly difficult, because our appetites increased due to the bitter cold. Apparently, the human body requires more calories in winter in order to stay warm.

Here is yet another example of trying to obtain food. When I arrived at work on the cold morning of January 1, 1944, one of my coworkers, Kretchmer, a glazier by profession who was old enough to be my father, approached me. He told me that the day before, he had noticed a fairly large group of officers getting ready for their New Year's party at a certain nearby house. Kretchmer was sure that the officers had gotten drunk at the party and were still sleeping it off. Therefore, he believed that it was very likely that we could find significant amounts of leftover food and drink still on the tables. He suggested that we take the chance and head over there on the pretext that we had come to do glasswork.

I did not hesitate for a second. I grabbed a wooden box filled with glass-cutting tools that I had found nearby and joined Kretchmer, who was carrying similar equipment. We walked toward the officers' spacious hall, located on the first floor of a two-story house at the end of the main road, which bisected the airfield. We were worried that the front door would be locked. Kretchmer told me that if we were seen, it would appear as if we had come to work. He stressed that we must act confidently and not display any signs of fear or hesitation. With quickened steps and beating hearts, we arrived at our destination.

We immediately noticed that the front door was wide open. Without thinking, we entered quickly, and our eyes took in the dozens of tables, covered with full bottles of wine, brandy, beer, and other drinks, and platters holding leftover meats, fish, vegetables, fruits and other delicacies such as cookies, biscuits, and even plenty of candy.

I felt as if I were dreaming. For a moment, we stood still, stunned and at a loss. We had to decide where to begin because time was of the essence. Subconsciously, we realized that we had to work swiftly, gather as much food as possible, and then make a hasty escape. Obviously, we did not touch the drinks, because they did not interest us. We quickly placed whatever food we could reach, a little bit of everything, into our boxes. After a few short minutes, we agreed that it was enough and that we had to get away from that intoxicating place.

Suddenly, we heard the gruff voice of a German officer, "What are you doing here?!"

Panicked and terrified, we ran out of the open backdoor without uttering a word. Kretchmer, the glazier, turned right, and I went left toward the street. My heart beat in fear and dread. I looked back and saw that the German officer had removed his pistol from his belt and was aiming it at me.

Instinctively, my feet began to run faster. It was as if some hidden power was pulling me forward. As I ran back to my workplace, I zigzagged around the houses. My main concern during those terrifying moments was that the German officer would shoot me. In order to protect myself, I kept glancing backward to check if he could still see me. When I was satisfied that he was no longer visible, I relaxed somewhat and slowed down.

When I got closer to my workplace, I stopped running. I took a deep breath and told myself, with much satisfaction: In spite of the stress and the fear that I had just experienced, I still managed to obtain some food for myself.

And thus, for me, the new civil year—1944—began with a fear of starvation and a hunt for food.

I did not know what the German officer was thinking. Did he mean to scare me or did he really intend to shoot me? I decided that I could not count on his conscience, determination, or thoughts. Rather, I had to escape and disappear as soon as possible. Once again, I realized that we were waging a brutal war of survival and that there was no limit to the risks we were willing to take.

The sad and tragic end of Pruskauer, the electrician from Czechoslovakia

One winter morning in early 1944, as we walked out of Spilve's gate on our way to work, we learned that one Jew from our company had been missing during morning roll call: Pruskauer, the electrician from Czechoslovakia.

Although we continued to work as we did on every weekday—on Sundays, we stayed in the camp to rest—we were amazed and impressed by Pruskauer's valiant spirit and courageous heart. He had realized and carried out his dream of fleeing the Nazis' talons. In an unfamiliar and hostile environment, unable to speak Latvian (the local language), and without worrying that he would be identified, he nevertheless dared to try and escape to freedom. We all prayed that he would succeed, and we hoped that the Nazis would not catch him.

But fate would have it otherwise. Several days later, when we returned from work, we learned that he had been captured and brought back to the camp. The Jews who had remained in camp that day told us that the SS sentenced Pruskauer to death. He was hanged in an empty room near headquarters, which served as a storeroom. Abba Tzapp, the SS-appointed overseer, was forced to watch as the victim breathed his last. Those dramatic days with their bitter end greatly affected the mood of the Jews in Spilve, especially those who worked in Pruskauer's company. He was very popular and well liked by all who knew him.

The SS-appointed overseers are replaced

During that winter, the Spilve commanders were replaced twice. A fat German of Swiss origin replaced Gustav Sorge, the brutal commander. Thanks to the new commander, the conditions in the camp improved somewhat, and the tension eased up a bit.

Often, on Sundays, we would walk to HKP, a labor camp that was located a few kilometers away to enjoy the concerts that the camp's Jewish inmates would hold for our mutual benefit.

Most of the prisoners at HKP were technicians such as car mechanics, locksmiths, and welders, who served the German Army by fixing and repairing different types of vehicles. There were also several famous musicians such as Tchuzoy the accordionist, whose reputation preceded him in Riga's prewar musical world. He would often appear as a virtuoso soloist on the radio. After the concerts, which allowed us to forget our daily misery for a brief moment, we would return to Spilve.

The food rations were the same as they had been during Gustav Sorge's days. Thus, each one of us tried, to the best of our abilities and talents, to use various schemes to find an additional source of food. We were not always successful.

The camp's new commander had a favorite pastime. He had a particular weakness for young, pretty women. After an initial selection during the daily roll calls, he would invite, via various Jewish intermediaries from the camp, young girls and women to spend time with him at night.

It was specifically during his term as camp commander that there was a suicide, something which had not occurred previously.

A middle-aged man who belonged to our labor company—his brother was Levitt, the carpenter from Riga—hung himself, apparently from despair and bitter desperation.

A young man named Monastirsky, who lived on our floor, found an opportune moment to escape Spilve. We learned of his intentions the evening before his daring escape. Many of us, including our overseer Abba Tzapp and his family, organized a farewell gathering for him. We sang and wished him much success. Apparently, he had good and special connections outside Spilve. During the following days, we did not know what happened to him. This incident took place during the time that the Nazi Gustav Sorge commanded the camp, and we could not begin to imagine what sort of punishment we would receive. Yet, fortunately and surprisingly, everything ended well. It was as if it never happened. No one even mentioned it.

When spring arrived, a new SS officer took command of our labor camp. He was older, in his sixties, and short. In a gruff voice, yet not in a commanding tone, he introduced himself to us during evening roll call on the day he took over from his predecessor. He told us that we must be obedient and follow all of the SS officers' orders. He added that if, for instance, we were told to leave Spilve when necessary, we must obey and comply, even if we were ordered to reach Honolulu (as he put it).

From this statement, we understood that the German Army was suffering defeats on the Soviet front and that there was a possibility that, together with our captors, we would be forced to retreat westward. Where exactly, we could not guess.

One thing was clear. None of the SS officers, who commanded us as if we were a reasonable labor force, would want to leave us, lest they be drafted and sent to the front. They were all acutely aware of their situation and knew that they could be "heroes" only when their weapons were aimed at weak and frail people like us, who had no way of defending themselves.

Meanwhile, there were no significant changes in our daily routine in camp, even during the new commander's reign. Shortly after his arrival, about seven hundred men and women from our camp were transferred to the city of Ponevezh. They all went willingly. Perhaps they considered the famous saying, "One who changes his location, changes his fate."

I was not excited about this and acted with restraint. When the new SS officer took over as camp commander, headquarters decided to conduct a thorough and top-secret inspection of all our wings. I heard about it the day before. My concerns grew because of my unnumbered spare work suit (overall) that was hidden under the straw mattress on my bed. I deliberated what to do, because I still hoped that there would be a good opportunity to use the overall to escape without arousing suspicion.

The next day, it occurred to me to hide it in the room belonging to our Jewish overseer (Tzapp and his family), because I assumed that his room would not be searched. I went to his room and asked him if I could leave it there until that evening after work. He immediately agreed. I placed the overall in a far corner underneath one of the beds. Relieved and pleased with my successful idea, I reported to work as on every other day. But first,

I collected all the pages of my journal, which I had rewritten from memory about everything that had happened from the beginning of the war through my time in Spilve, and threw them down the toilet.

At 6:00 p.m., as I was returning to the camp with my labor company, I noticed Abba Tzapp approaching me from a distance, his eyes gleaming with anger and rage. I realized that something had happened. He told me to wait for him to come back and meanwhile not to return to my room. I knew that I was in for an unpleasant experience.

When the rest of my labor company had gone back to their respective rooms, Abba Tzapp came over and stood in front of me without saying a word. At that moment, I was sure that there were no SS men in the area, but Tzapp knew for a fact that they were there. He desperately wanted to find favor in their eyes and to show them that he too could punish Jews when necessary. He raised his strong right hand and punched me, hard. The pain was so intense that I saw sparks.

Stunned, I asked him, "Abba, why do I deserve this? Answer me!"

He replied resolutely, "You yourself know the answer!"

I whispered back, "Know, that when the day comes and we're liberated, I will settle this debt."

When I returned to my room, and everyone saw my red, swollen cheek, they were very upset by Tzapp's despicable action. But I later learned that the Germans had conducted rigorous searches of every room, which housed Jewish prisoners, with no exceptions, including the Tzapp family's room. It was there that they had found my overall. I realized that if I had been punished by the Germans themselves, I would have been much worse off.

After this incident, when I no longer had an unnumbered overall (because they never returned it to me), I decided to swim with the current. Whatever happened to everyone else would happen to me too. I would rely on my instincts during danger, when sharpened senses would show me how to survive, as they did during those terrible days in the prison, the ghetto, and the fortress in Dvinsk.

In May 1944, a sizeable number of women and young girls from Hungary were brought to Spilve. Until Passover of that year, they had been living in their own homes, like every other citizen of that country. They did not appear to be starving, but they were frightened. Compared to the suffering and bitter fate of the other Jews in Nazi-occupied Europe, the tribulations of these Hungarian women were relatively minor. Most of these women, who came from cities and villages, were religious. Nearly all of them had prayer books, the only things they had taken with them when they were deported to the unknown. They had tried to stick together on the way to Riga, and they were afraid that they would be separated. They literally held on tightly to each other's hands. The spectacle was extremely moving.

In addition to Hungarian, they also spoke German and a bit of *Galitzianer*-accented Yiddish. There were young girls among them, and some of the women were very beautiful. We were all worried lest they fall into the SS men's filthy hands.

The Hungarian group was housed in the place where the seven hundred Jews who had been sent to the labor camp in Ponevezh, Lithuania, had previously been housed. Tzapp's wife was in charge of these women, and Tzapp continued to be in charge of the men.

Shortly before Passover, the SS had replaced Metzger, the Jewish overseer from Germany, with a Jew named Reiken. Young, tall, and very good-looking, Reiken was brought from another labor camp. We did not know where Metzger was sent, but Reiken shared Metzger's fate. A short time later, he simply disappeared, and we never heard from him again.

Meanwhile, the Tzapps stayed where they were. When the two of them, especially the wife, noticed the Hungarians' different and unfamiliar lifestyle, they started to abuse the poor women. They tried to discipline them with shouts and reprimands, and the women were terrified. It was difficult to see their scared faces.

To those of us who had become accustomed to the countless agonies and torments, the Tzapps's attitude and treatment of the wretched women seemed strange and unnatural. We could not understand how Jews could behave with cruelty and degradation toward other Jews, even if they wanted to find favor in the Nazis' eyes. However, a Nazi overseer would have treated the women even worse.

Eventually, the women were sent to hard physical labor near the airfield where Jewish women from our labor camp used to work. They all shared the same bitter and cruel fate. One day, those unfortunate women disappeared, and we never saw them again.

According to the rumors we heard, they were put to death by the Nazis, who had received an order from on high.

The warfront approaches

In the middle of the summer of 1944, we learned from various sources that the battlefront was drawing near, and our mood improved by the day. Yet, subconsciously, we worried and felt restless about our unknown future. What was in store for us?

Little by little, the first signs of the situation on the fronts started to appear in our immediate area. The Germans became irritable and were no longer as sure of themselves or their triumphs on the European and Soviet fronts as they had been in the not too distant past.

Following the Allied armies' long-awaited crossing of the English Channel in early June, a second front had opened in the West, and the Allies began to attack and threaten the German Army's well-oiled war machine. At times, it seemed as if the end of the war was growing closer, as the Allied armies advanced to Germany's prewar border. We also heard rumors from the Soviet front that the German army of occupation was constantly retreating all along that vast front. Cities and small towns in eastern Lithuania had already been liberated from the Nazi Army, including my birthplace, Utian!

Our labor company's German overseer, a civilian engineer named Schmidt, started to assemble and send various packages filled with war spoils to his family in Konigsberg, East Prussia. I would write the addresses on these packages.

One summer day, as we were working, we heard a long siren. It was an omen that Soviet bombers were attacking Riga. For us, the slave laborers, it was like the most beautiful music. It exhilarated our souls and lifted our spirits.

Obviously, our path to freedom was far from over, but nevertheless, everyone, myself included, hoped for the best. I also hoped that once this terrible war and all its difficult experiences ended, I would have the privilege of seeing my sisters whom I missed so much.

As I was contemplating the future, one of my friends from work showed me the wagon driver and the wagon that brought us the mud-colored, watery soup every day at noon. Together with my friends from work, I went out to meet it and saw the following scene: German officers and soldiers, who had heard the alarm and the siren, were running in confusion—fear and dread in their eyes—to find shelter in the airfield's underground cellars, which the Germans had built for this purpose.

Instinctively, I started running with them, but I noticed that they paid no attention to me. I descended with them into the nearest cellar and stayed there until the Russian airplanes had finished doing what they were supposed to do. That is, they bombed certain targets and then returned to their base. I was the only Jew there.

I did not miss my soup, because the wagon driver knew how many portions he was supposed to distribute. Later that day, when we were tired from work and had just fallen asleep, we were awakened by the frightening sound of aerial bombings over Riga. I got out of bed and looked out the window to see what was going on outside. The sky was lit up like the day from the illumination flares that the Russians had set off to hit their targets with precision. The bombing continued until well past midnight.

We could not fall asleep after the "show." My head was filled with countless thoughts about the near future. In our imaginations, we could already savor the sweet taste of liberation from Spilve by the advance units of the Red Army, which continued to attack the German Army all along the entire front, from East to West.

But then, inevitably, came the unwelcome thought, "What if, God forbid, we missed the train…"

Desperately, I tried to force myself to ignore those misgivings and doubts about my ability to survive the inferno. I held on to a small ray of hope and tenaciously believed that a brighter morning would arrive someday. Yet, since it was clear that I could not rely solely on miracles, I looked for a real opportunity to actualize my dream.

A group of young Jews in their twenties from Kovno had been working for an extended period of time in the forests several dozen kilometers north of Riga. They were charged with chopping down trees, and they lived in tents. This group referred to itself as the "woodcutters company" ("*Holzkommando*" in German). Every so often, members of this company would come to our labor camp, escorted by German guards, in order to obtain food for their daily needs. By chance, I once met a young Jew from Utian, who worked as a barber for that company. I asked him to submit a request to the Germans so that I could go work with them, and he promised that he would do so. Later, the Sheffer brothers from Kovno, who knew my good friend Lumiansky from before the war, also promised that they would submit a request.

I believed that if I would be located farther away from Riga and not constantly under the SS men's eyes, I would have a better chance of escaping and surviving. Each day, I hoped that I would hear that they needed an additional worker. And, in fact, such an opportunity arose, and I was convinced that I would be going to work in the forest. I was on the list of workers, and I was supposed to go there the next morning. I could not sleep that night because I was certain that my dream was coming true. But at daybreak, I discovered that the Germans had chosen someone else, a young man from Germany, to go work with them. He obviously spoke German better than I did, and apparently, this was important to the Germans.

Meanwhile, when the Nazis realized that the ground had started to burn beneath their feet, that their day of reckoning was approaching, and that they would have to answer to humanity for their wartime crimes, they initiated a unique project. With the help of Jews from the labor camps and Red Army prisoners of war, they disinterred from the mass graves in and around Riga the bodies of the Jews and the prisoners of war who had been tortured and savagely put to death. These bodies were then burned to ashes.

The idea was to ensure that there would be neither living witnesses nor evidence of the mass killings. When the Nazis had committed their crimes, they had assumed that they would never have to relinquish the countries they had occupied and that they would never have to justify their actions to the world. But now that time was no longer on their side, they launched this ghastly project with great secrecy.

Within a few days, however, we started to hear reports of their diabolical deeds. They brought a certain number of Jews and non-Jews from the labor camps to the pits. These prisoners were housed in tents under inhumane conditions, and around the clock they were forced to remove the bodies from the mass graves and then burn them in a massive bonfire.

The resultant unbearable stench spread over a radius that was many kilometers wide and raised the locals' suspicions that something unusual was happening nearby. The Nazis referred to the site where they cremated their victims' bodies as *Stützpunkt* (base).

SS men came from Kaiserwald to draft men from our labor camp to that accursed place. We all realized that no one would return from there alive, and so nobody volunteered to go. Therefore, the Nazis took anyone SS Headquarters had designated as a "criminal"—in other words, one who had broken one of the Germans' disciplinary rules. According to the SS, if a Jew was caught trading or bartering food within the camp or trading valuables for food with Christians outside the camp, that was considered to be a "serious crime."

Once, an entire company of Jews was sent to the Stützpunkt because they dared to sing an inspirational Soviet song as they returned to camp after a long and difficult day of work.

The tension in the camp increased immeasurably when on a late autumn evening, just before dusk, the SS doctor from Kaiserwald arrived together with a number of officers. We were all very concerned about the reason for their arrival. Short and bespectacled, the SS doctor ordered all the Jews in the camp to line up for a second roll call at about 6:00 p.m. After examining the tally and consulting with the camp's overseers, he went from person to person, asking about our health and if we were sick.

Obviously, none of us even considered complaining about our health, because we knew what being sick meant in an SS labor camp.

The next day, the SS guards began carrying out the doctor's orders. Actually, the "doctor" was an "expert" on selections—who would live and who would die. In the morning, our entire company left for work, as on every other day. When we returned to camp in the evening around 6:00, those who were still alive told us what had happened before their very eyes during that terrible day.

First, they forcefully separated the children from their anxious and frightened mothers and threw them into the trucks, which the SS had prepared for this purpose, like one tosses rags and dusters. The murderers gave a choice to any mother who dared to resist by force and to protect her child: She could either stay in the camp without her children or else join them. Some of the mothers went to their deaths with their children.

Until that fateful day, the number of children in the camp was relatively small because they had gone through numerous selections from the beginning of the war until they arrived in Spilve. We were all encouraged by the fact that there were still Jewish children in our midst, and we hoped that they were destined for a better future, one without misery or suffering. But when we learned the terrible truth, we were despondent and horrified, because there were no longer any children in the camp. They had all been taken to their deaths, together with several mothers who refused to abandon them.

We could not find words to console the parents or the lonely mothers, who had already lost their husbands. Their children had been brutally snatched from their arms forever.

One of the victims was the Tzapps's adorable four-year-old daughter. We all loved her. She would wander into our rooms and entertain us. As far as we were concerned, this proved that the German murderers did not even have consideration or compassion for the Jews who served them obediently on a daily basis in various administrative roles within the camp.

Before we had a chance to calm down after the catastrophic loss of the poor Jewish children, yet another calamity occurred. Once again, the same doctor, the "selection specialist," arrived and requested that the camp's administration provide him with a list of the camp's Jewish inmates who were over fifty years old. The next day, all of the "older" Jews remained in the camp.

Even a number of Jews from our labor company were forced to stay behind with the murderers on that fateful day, including Shimon Kagan the tinsmith, my best friend Shaymeh Lumiansky, and Plutkin the carpenter. Needless to say, we did not expect to hear good news when we returned to camp. Thus, I was greatly surprised and overjoyed to find Lumiansky in my room, alive and well. However, my coworker Meyeran, Kagan the tinsmith, and Plutkin the carpenter were all gone. May their memories be blessed.

Lumiansky told me how he ended up alive, and I was stunned by his dramatic story. Here is how he described what took place in the camp:

> "The SS-appointed overseer ordered all the older Jews in camp out of their rooms. After they lined up in a single row, they waited, anxiously and fearfully, for the 'specialist doctor' from Kaiserwald to speak. He had arrived at that time and counted the Jews. The tension continued to increase as the 'specialist' moved along the line and examined each and every man's face with his murderous and penetrating gaze. Without saying a word, he reached the end of the row and stood in front of me. He asked me how old I was. When I told him that I was fifty years old, he deliberated for a moment and said that he was willing to test my physical fitness. He ordered someone to bring him a long table and placed it several meters in front of me.
>
> "He then said, 'This is your moment of truth. You must prove, in practical terms, that you're physically fit.'
>
> "I was flabbergasted by his words, and then he continued, 'You must jump over the table without touching it!'
>
> "I was certain that if I did not accomplish this task, I would be facing a death sentence. (He boasted to me that in his youth, he had been involved in various winter and summer sports.) Mustering all my strength for that fateful task which could determine my fate, I stepped back a bit, and in a daring jump, I managed to leap over the table with about a meter and a half to spare!

"And then I fell to the ground. As I got up, unassisted, the local SS men and the 'specialist' were surprised by the results of the athletic show that had been organized for their amusement. They ordered me to stand on the side, and then I realized that I had successfully passed the test of my life…for the meantime."

The Battle for the Riga Road

In early September 1944 we heard encouraging news, which lifted our spirits. We read in the Latvian and German papers, which we happened to find, that the German Army was retreating rapidly to the West along the entire eastern front. In addition, we knew that since June, the American and British armies had been advancing into Germany. The eastern part of Latvia, including Dvinsk, was already in the Red Army's hands, and central and eastern Lithuania had been liberated as well. For some time, fierce battles continued to rage around the strategically located city of Shavli; the Germans knew that if the Russians should capture the city, Germany's fortunes would take a turn for the worse.

As the front neared Riga, a mere forty kilometers to the south, we felt that our fates would also soon be decided. Reverberations of artillery battles reached our ears from the city of Boisk, which was still in German hands. Around the clock, we heard sirens, as ambulances carried the wounded to Riga's military hospitals.

We sensed that the SS administrators were unsure how to proceed. They awaited instructions from their superiors about what to do next. Meanwhile, we continued to work as usual in the airfield, since we had not received any orders to the contrary from the camp's SS overseers.

On Sunday morning, September 24, when we went to the camp's courtyard, we suddenly heard an announcement over the loudspeaker from the commander: "A decision has been made to transfer you from Spilve back to Kaiserwald."

Shortly thereafter, we were given food rations for the trip, including, to our great surprise, cigarettes! The SS men's attitude toward us underwent a complete change. Not a single nasty word escaped their lips!

In private discussions, we concluded that this change in attitude was a manifestation of the German Army's losses on the fronts. And should the situation deteriorate even further, even the SS men would probably be drafted and sent to the front to fight against the Russians. Hence, they preferred to deal with us in the concentration camps in the rear and to bind their fates to ours. On a personal level, they would all be better off this way. But in any event, their self-confidence decreased drastically.

All the Jews in Spilve were ordered, according to an announcement that came over the loudspeaker, to report immediately to the camp's courtyard. The Germans allowed us to bring the food rations we had received as well as the cigarettes and several other small personal items. As soon as we had assembled, the SS men, led by their commander, ordered us to start marching to the Daugava River.

After a long, tiring march, we finally reached the river, where we boarded a ship, which carried us to Kaiserwald.

At Kaiserwald, it was as if nothing had happened in the intervening year. We were immediately sent to the cold bathhouses. After we bathed in cold water without soap, they confiscated our numbered civilian clothes and replaced them with black-and-white striped cotton uniforms with matching hats. We were allowed to keep our shoes. The numbers that served as our identity cards appeared on the left side of our jackets.

Next, we were taken to the barracks, which were furnished only with wooden bunk beds, without mattresses, pillows, or blankets. Our new commanders showed us where to place our meager belongings, except for our food and cigarettes, which we took with us. We were led to a large field, and after receiving a bit of watery soup for lunch—the same soup that they would give us in Spilve—we were ordered to run. The weather was wintry, cold, and rainy. We were forced to run in circles, back and forth, until nightfall. By that time, we had exhausted whatever strength we still (surprisingly) had left.

When we returned to the barracks, we were given some of the same type of bread we had received in Spilve, together with a bit of margarine and a cup of unsweetened coffee. Exhausted from the running, we had no problem falling asleep on the bare bunks.

The next day, Monday, September 25, we were once again forced to run in circles, exposed to the bitter cold. Twice that day we received our usual starvation rations. Fortunately, we all still had some food left from Spilve and used that to supplement our meager rations.

Before darkness fell, the new SS officers ordered us to prepare for our departure from Kaiserwald. We were to go, on foot, of course, to Riga's port.

We walked together with Jews, from other labor camps, who had been brought like us to Kaiserwald. From Riga, we were to travel westward by ship over the Baltic Sea, but our final destination was unknown to us. As we walked, the SS guards forced us to maintain a brisk pace.

After walking for several kilometers, we reached the port where we stood at attention before a military cargo ship. We waited to board because we knew that there was nowhere else to go.

Everything looked black (except for the brightly lit cargo ship) —the somber winter sky, the stormy sea, the strong winds. A blackout engulfed the city of Riga as a precaution against aerial attacks. Even our souls were overwhelmed by gloom and darkness. We could not prevent the SS from carrying out their scheme of deporting us from Latvia westward, from using us for their nefarious, personal goals and as cheap fuel for Hitler's well-oiled war machine.

Thus ends my time in Riga, on my way to liberation.

CHAPTER SIX:

Retreat via the Baltic Sea and the Stutthof Concentration Camp

The port of Riga was packed with people, vehicles, and assorted equipment that had been removed from the various factories around Riga. The SS units were to transfer the equipment to Germany and to use the Jewish labor force for their military objectives. And at the same time, the SS men could thus avoid being sent to the front.

Just before noon, we were ordered aboard and were quickly thrown deep down into the ship's bowels. When we looked outside, the ship seemed to be quite large. We figured that there would be plenty of room for us and that we would be comfortable. However, many more people continued to arrive, and we could no longer stretch out on our backs. We were forced to lie on our sides instead of sitting on the metal surfaces of the ship's lower decks. Each person tried to get settled without bothering his neighbors on either side.

Most of us still had some food left from the rations we had received that morning in Kaiserwald. The SS commanders, led by Zauer, Hoffmann, and Schiller, were left with a large stock of food in their warehouses, and since they could not possibly take it all with them, they acted with generosity and increased our rations.

While on board the ship, I bumped into Klezmer, a Jewish glazier, who had worked with me in the Riga airfield. He was in his sixties, but he was energetic, optimistic, and filled with joie de vivre. We lay next to each other. He tried to raise everyone's morale. A woman lay on the other side of him, because there were both men and women on the ship's lower decks. However, in the deck above us, there were only women, and the ship's crew, the SS commanders, and the guards were housed in the upper decks in separate cabins under much better conditions.

The day the ship sailed out of Riga was Yom Kippur. One could hear soft, tearful prayers emanating from every corner of the ship.

For the next three days and nights, the ship rocked over the stormy waves. Those of us on the lower decks felt it strongly. Every once in a while, we received a bit of bread and water. The lack of oxygen and the stench from our sweaty clothes were unbearable.

The SS men would briefly open the covering to let in some air. When the people nearest the opening asked the SS men to leave it open for longer, they would slam it closed, deliberately and spitefully. Once, someone asked for water to drink. In response, the SS men took a bucket of water, uncovered the opening, and poured the water on the thirsty Jews' heads.

Finally, when we reached the port of Gdansk, the stormy sea quieted down. The ship came to a halt, and they opened the entrance. The sun's rays blinded us. After three days on the ship, during which nearly all of us suffered from seasickness, emotional stress, and a lack of oxygen and water, the horrible nightmare finally ended.

As fast as we could, we ran ashore toward the dock and the concourse. Breathing in the fresh air under the SS guards' watchful eyes, we formed a semicircle on a wide field.

Surprisingly, the SS men and the ship's crew allowed us to return to the ship to take the leftover food from the tables in their cabins. Together with some other guys who were about my age, I volunteered for this mission. Within a short while, after making a few trips to the ship, we had managed to collect a significant amount of good food, such as we had not seen or tasted in ages, for ourselves and for our starving, downtrodden brothers.

While waiting for orders from the SS commanders, I had plenty of time to speak to some of my acquaintances from the ghetto and the fortress in Dvinsk, Latvia. It had been over a year since we had last met.

I tried to give them as much of the food from the ship as I could. We were all thrilled to see each other again. Each person had his own story to tell. We had suffered just as much during the past year as we had during the previous two years. Out of the three hundred people whom the Germans had deported by train from

Dvinsk to Riga in late October 1943, I met no more than a few dozen.

I was especially sorry that my good friend Baruch Kwill from Kraslava, Latvia, was not there. We had survived all the aktions in the Dvinsk ghetto together. In addition, we had seen each other on a daily basis in the fortress until we were separated on November 7, 1943, in Kaiserwald. When I was sent to Spilve, he was sent to Dundagen. No one could tell me what had happened to him. I was comforted by the hope that perhaps he had managed to survive.

Relatively speaking, we enjoyed those few hours. We had the rare opportunity to wander freely around the concourse while savoring the fresh air and late autumn sun as well as meeting and talking to our friends.

The crew had left the port and gone on their way, and the SS commanders were apparently busy planning how to transport us to the Stutthof concentration camp. The guards kept their eyes on us, but they did not disturb us.

We knew nothing about Stutthof.

At long last, we were ordered to line up and start walking toward the Vistula River. When we reached the shore, we saw the barges that were to carry us to our destination. Suddenly, the sky grew dark, and by the time we had crowded on to the barges, it had begun to rain. As far as I can recall, we were covered with a tarpaulin roof. However, the sides were open, and there were strong gusts of wind. We were all soaked.

The barges were attached to each other with bridges, which allowed the guards to move from barge to barge to maintain order, to distribute food, and so on. But to the best of my recollection, the guards did not pay much attention to us. The SS officers kept their distance and used binoculars and a loudspeaker.

Not too far from me in the barge was one of my old friends from the Dvinsk ghetto. His name was Efraim Kobb, and he was about fifty years old. He was a native of my hometown of Utian, and I knew his entire family. As I mentioned above, he and his family adopted my mother Liba Raizel—may Hashem avenge her blood—who became part of their family. Thus, Efraim was very close to my heart and was like a father to me. During one of the aktions in the ghetto, he lost his wife, daughter-in-law, and the rest of his family. Only his daughter was left to share his bitter fate.

I discussed our present circumstances and our murky future with him. Among other things, he noted that during World War I, he had been a soldier in the czar's army, and he had fought in this area around the Vistula River. He had been captured by the Germans, who had treated him humanely. This reminded me of something my mother had told me when I was a young child: My father had also fought in the czar's army and had been taken prisoner, but he managed to escape and return to his family.

I told him about his shoemaker friend from the fortress, who had tried but failed to commit suicide. He too was traveling with us to Stutthof.

The main difference between our voyage by ship from Riga to Gdansk and our voyage by barge along the Vistula River was that during the latter trip, we did not lack oxygen even though the barges were very crowded. We were not overly thirsty either. As we sailed, we noticed the beautiful view on either side of the wide river. The forests were awash in bright colors, especially orange-yellow, a sure sign of autumn.

Our clothes were thin and tattered, and we were concerned about the rapidly approaching winter. Yet, in my heart, I consoled myself with the following idea: If the SS leadership had wanted to get rid of us, they could have easily done so in occupied Latvia. And since they did not do so, I reasoned, it was a sign that we were still indispensable to them. But liberation from their blood-soaked talons was still far off, and we were in desperate need of a miracle.

After sailing along the Vistula River for several hours, we were ordered to climb ashore and line up. Under heavy guard, we were led to Stutthof. On the way, we passed a village of well-tended, white houses surrounded by various types of flowers. We did not know who lived in those houses, but we noticed Jewish women working in the gardens. I was able to exchange a few words with one of them. She hastily told me, without attracting the guards' notice, that the women had arrived in Stutthof by train in early July. They had been deported from the Kovno ghetto after its liquidation.

We passed the village and reached the camp's entrance. A sign in German read *WALDLAGER STUTTHOF* (STUTTHOF FOREST CAMP) so that the newly arrived prisoners would not know what awaited them in reality. Some of the camp's commanders arrived and told us that we were now in a place where one must forget one's past, alter one's true identity, and obey orders. The women were immediately separated from the men.

We were then sent to the showers. The showers were cold and very quick, and we were given neither soap nor towels. Afterward, we received striped uniforms with matching hats and heavy, open, wooden shoes. Luckily and surprisingly, they did not beat us as they distributed the clothing and the shoes, but we sensed that we were not in for a rosy future. Each man had a number on his jacket. I had the same number as I had in Kaiserwald: 96027.

We saw rectangular barracks (known as "blocks"), and hundreds of prisoners, not all of whom were Jewish, crowded and idled nearby. Our block was Block 3, which faced the Poles' block. Their dim expressions and downcast eyes, as if they were searching for something on the ground, revealed the dismal truth about this hellish camp.

Cautiously, when no one was watching, they told us that here in this ghastly camp, every prisoner had to beware of the *kapos* (criminal prisoners who were responsible for maintaining order inside and outside the block and other administrative tasks). The kapos were particularly brutal when the SS men were nearby.

For a long while, we crowded around outside our block. Suddenly, several sadistic-looking Poles appeared and introduced themselves as the kapos who were in charge of us. In execrable German, they explained the camp's daily schedule: After hearing the bell, we had to report for roll call twice a day, in the morning and in the evening. After the morning roll call, we would be given only black coffee; at noon, there would be some sort of watery soup with a few cabbage leaves or grains of barley; and following the evening roll call, we would be given a mere 150-200 grams of bread.

At about 6:00 p.m., the bell (known as the "gong" in the camp) started to ring, and we all ran to line up in two long rows for roll call before the SS officers came and counted us. Casually, for no apparent reason, the officers struck anyone who was standing in a way that they did not like. As always, they tried to frighten us and threatened that those who did not obey orders would be put to death.

We were then ordered to wait for the bread to be distributed. After standing in line for a long time, we finally received our bread and were allowed to enter the barracks.

One of us, a Jew from Kovno, was put in charge of the latrine. The SS ordered him to maintain cleanliness and to allow several men into the latrine at once, by turn. This caused particular hardship for those who suffered from digestive or urinary ailments. However, one could not complain or beseech the kapo, because the consequences would be catastrophic—a direct ride by wagon to the gas chambers and the crematoriums, which operated around the clock at full capacity.

The barracks contained three-story bunk beds, which were insufficient for the number of prisoners. Thus, we were forced to sleep, in our clothes and wooden shoes, under extremely crowded conditions. Due to the lack of space, some men even stretched out under the bunks.

I found a spot on a lower bunk, near the door. This way, I would be able to exit quickly in case we were to receive sudden orders from the SS commander. Due to exhaustion and emotional turmoil, I fell asleep immediately. I was awakened at 6:00 a.m. by the morning roll call gong, which was accompanied by the Polish kapos' menacing shouts: *"Prentko!"* ("Hurry!"). We were not permitted to use the latrine, which was, needless to say, very distressing.

When the roll call was over, we were each given unsweetened black coffee and divided into labor groups. In fact, the "labor" was actually a means of satisfying the sadistic urges of the German overseers and the Polish kapos. Later, the Jewish laborers told the rest of us that they had been compelled via severe beatings to move giant piles of sand, using cement sacks made out of paper, while running frantically back and forth. The rest of the day had been comprised of similar contrivances, which were all designed to break their spirit and strength.

I stayed near the barracks that day together with many other Jews from Block 3. I searched for Efraim Kobb, my older friend from Utian, and his fellow shoemaker, Chaim, as well as several of my other close friends from Dvinsk. Some of them had been sent to labor, but I happened to meet Efraim. His mood had deteriorated dramatically. During the course of our long talk that day, I deliberately touched upon a basic question: Would our lives have any meaning—even if we were somehow to make it through the inferno to freedom at the end of the war—after having lost all our loved ones? He considered my question with cold logic and answered with the following words, which I have not forgotten:

"I, personally, am unsure if I'll be able to rebuild myself, should I ever be liberated. But you're only twenty-three years old, and you certainly would be able to build your future from the ground up."

We also discussed many other important topics. His encouraging words invigorated me and strengthened my faith in life and my hope that the Germans would lose the war.

At this point, I must share a barbaric incident that took place that day before my very eyes. I shall never forget it. While they were distributing the soup near the Polish block, I suddenly heard terrible cries. The reason for this was that the Polish kapo, who was present when the prisoners received their rations, noticed, correctly or mistakenly, that one of the prisoners had lined up to receive a second portion.

And this is when the show began. Like a wild animal, the sadistic kapo attacked the wretched prisoner who could barely stand on his own feet as it was. After shoving him to the ground, the kapo kicked him over his entire body and did not stop until the man breathed his last.

The kapos would force the prisoners to wander around the camp with a wagon to collect the dead and the half-dead, who had been taken to the crematorium after being gassed to death. We quickly realized that we must persevere and not show any sign of physical weakness, lest we be sent directly to the gas chamber.

During my stay in Stutthof, I witnessed a group of Jewish women, who had come from the Lodz ghetto after it was liquidated, being led on foot to the gas chamber. They looked like human shadows, horrifically thin and barely able to move as they met their end.

Once, on a cold and rainy night, we were all awakened and ordered to report immediately to the camp's main square where we were forced to watch a young Polish man's execution. He had tried to escape but was caught and sentenced to death by hanging. We were shocked to see how the hangman did his work dispassionately and with complete indifference. After we were sent back to the barracks, I was too upset to fall asleep.

Apparently, the SS commanders hoped to remain in Stutthof for the duration of the winter. Therefore, as the chilly days and nights approached, they decided to have the kapos and the many prisoners who could still do hard labor store the potatoes in their underground storerooms. This time, I was unable to elude the Polish kapos who had assembled numerous work groups for this hard physical labor. While shouting "Prentko!" they forced us to run with wheelbarrows filled with potatoes to the underground storerooms. Using all my physical and emotional strength, I was able to complete the task to the kapos' satisfaction and thus avoided a beating. Luckily, this was the only labor I did in the ghastly, hellish Stutthof concentration camp. Although I was there over a month, I worked for only about a week.

When the work was finished, I was sent to the railway, which was located outside the camp, to sort the murdered victims' shoes. As it turned out, this job worked to my advantage. I worked alone in a train car, without being watched by the kapos or the SS men. Only the scattered shoes spoke to me and told me the tragic, melancholy tale of their owners, who had met their bitter fate in that accursed camp.

In the giant heap of shoes, I found a pair my size. Without hesitating, I removed my wooden shoes and buried them deep in the large pile of shoes. I thus obtained a complete pair of heavy shoes, which would enable me to continue my life in the concentration camp.

The next day, after roll call and breakfast, the prisoners in our barracks heard a rumor that the Germans were organizing groups of prisoners with various occupations, especially metalworkers, to be transported to a labor camp in a factory in central Germany. Approximately five hundred men and women were required. No one knew the exact destination, but I had a gut feeling that I should take advantage of this opportunity, without knowing what type of work awaited me. The important thing was to get to Germany. My hope was that perhaps the Germans, who had hidden their terrible crimes in occupied Europe from their compatriots, would not treat us brutally in Germany itself.

When the moment of truth arrived and the camp's senior SS men announced over the loudspeaker that all the skilled workers must report immediately to the designated train cars, which would carry them to their destination, I went too. The cars were designed for transporting cargo and were open to the sky. Standing in place, we breathed in the fresh air, as the train began to move westward.

As I looked back, it occurred to me that it was good that I had dared to leave that accursed spot. Just thinking about that place is enough to make one shudder. I had willingly volunteered to go because I simply had nothing to lose. As I left Stutthof, I felt a tiny spark of hope that I would remain alive. However, I felt very sorry for all my acquaintances and dear friends, who remained in the bloodthirsty murderers' hands.

Shortly after we pulled away from the camp, I briefly glanced at an open cargo train like ours that was coming toward us. Suddenly, I found myself looking into the eyes of my dear friend from the Dvinsk ghetto: Shayna'le! I had not seen her since early November 1943, about a year before, in Kaiserwald. It seemed like a very long time to miss someone.

She was very thin and had a hopeless expression. My heart ached. All the women, most of them young, were crowded around her. I was consoled by the fact that she was still alive, and perhaps she would manage to survive the inferno.

For a long time afterward, her image remained with me, and my mind was flooded with memories. I remembered the period of our wonderful friendship and our plans for the future, if and when we should be liberated. We had encouraged each other to carry on and to overcome all the obstacles and hardships we were forced to endure. We shared many spiritual challenges. We had written songs and appeared together before our suffering brothers in the Dvinsk fortress. She would sing the songs she had written to Russian melodies, and I would accompany her on the mandolin.

Bitter reality soon forced me to abandon my dream and return to the present when I noticed the striped uniforms of the Jewish concentration camp inmates, including my own.

The open cargo train traveled on narrow tracks. When we arrived at a large train station after a short ride, we were transferred to bigger and closed cattle cars. Before we boarded, we were given food rations, which were reasonable compared to what we had been given in Stutthof, and the train left for Magdeburg.

CHAPTER SEVEN:

The Magdeburg Labor Camp

Our train ride from Stutthof to Magdeburg, a city in central Germany, on the banks of the Elbe River, lasted over twenty-four hours. When we finally arrived in the city in the evening, there were no lights in any of the windows. Only the train's headlights illuminated the way.

In Magdeburg's large train station, we were received by a delegation from the Polte factory accompanied by armed guards. We marched in rows of five. The Jewish women, who had been drafted for the same purpose in the Stutthof concentration camp, marched in front of us.

We soon arrived in the men's camp, which was located near the factory. The Jewish women who came with us were taken to a special camp—one of the many camps scattered throughout the vast complex—which also belonged to the Polte-Werke plant. A sign above the men's camp read: *"Koncetrations Lager Buchenwald – Ausenlager Magdeburg"* ("Buchenwald Concentration Camp – Magdeburg Subcamp").

Near the gate was a small structure with armed sentries, who guarded all the barbed-wire-enclosed labor camps in the complex.

Representatives of the plant arrived, wearing civilian clothing. They sorted the workers and sent them to the factory's different departments. I was selected to work in the department responsible for the final processing of artillery shell casings, using an electric metal-shaving machine.

I had a regular shift, from 6:00 p.m. to 6:00 a.m. During my shift, I had to file four hundred shells each day, without any defects. This difficult task was both mentally and physically demanding and required a great deal of concentration. My department head was a Nazi party official, who was meticulous about the product's quality.

I would finish off my food ration before arriving at work. At noon, we received watery vegetable soup and about two hundred grams of bread. By the time I would leave for work, I was already hungry. During my nighttime shift, I drank a great deal of unsweetened coffee without a crumb of food. I had a false sense of being full, but to my dismay, my legs became bloated from hunger.

Often during my stint in the shell-filing department, we were not allowed to go to sleep after completing our shifts. Instead, we were forced to clean the barracks or the courtyard. As a result of the sparse rations, the grueling work, and the lack of sleep, I felt as if my end was near. By late March 1945, I felt as if my feet could no longer hold me up. Desperate, I dared to ask my German overseers to transfer me to a different department with better conditions where I would not have to stand for twelve hours at a time.

However, my new job proved to be even worse. I was forced to remove glowing-hot casings from a giant metal oven, using a special tool and to transfer them immediately to a tub filled with liquid chemicals for cleaning and cooling. I worked with several other Jewish workers, but because of the steam from the chemicals, we could not see each other. The stench was unbearable.

After completing my shift, I told Pollack, our Jewish supervisor, that I could no longer stand up. The next day, I was transferred to the *Shonungsblock* (infirmary) for observation.

At this point, I will go back and recount what happened when we first arrived in the labor camp. Since we were all crawling with lice, we had to be disinfected (*Entlausung* in German), and, in the meantime, we were quarantined in our barracks for several days. When the quarantine period ended, we were taken to the bathhouse.

Afterward, in typical SS fashion, which, unfortunately, we knew quite well from Kaiserwald and Stutthof, we were given clean striped uniforms. Luckily, I was allowed to keep the shoes I had brought from Stutthof. These quality leather shoes were warm and sturdy, and they allowed me to survive the winter of 1945.

I was given a new number on the left side of my uniform: 96198.

While we were in quarantine, the sadistic SS men appointed Hoffmann and Schiller, who had come with us from Riga to Stutthof and then to Magdeburg, and Kagan, a Jewish prizefighter from Riga, as our overseers. Apparently, back in Kaiserwald, Kagan was considered to be the perfect man for this job. As the Jews who had been with him in Kaiserwald reported, he was known for his physical strength and his brutality toward his Jewish brothers. One of his blows to the face was sufficient to cause his victim to collapse.

Kagan was given a separate room off to the side of the barracks under much better conditions. He lived there with his younger, and more decent and humane, brother. The third man in their room was an honest, religious Jew from Germany, who was in charge of distributing food to the camp's inmates. His name was Vilner. He had three assistants: a Polish Jew named Eignetz in his early twenties, a Latvian Jew named Pollack, and a German Jew named Solomon. The three of them walked around with rubber sticks and terrified us. We were warned to avoid their beatings.

There were three barracks. I was in Barracks 3 where Eignetz was in charge. It was extremely crowded. The beds were three-story bunks, with a narrow passageway in between. Each man received a straw mattress and pillow as well as a thin blanket. Since it was wintertime, each barracks had a small wood-fed stove. However, the camp's German administrators did not permit us to light the stove every day. In addition, we were not allowed to use the stove for our own personal needs, such as cooking or frying the potatoes that we sometimes managed to obtain by various methods.

As I noted above, our daily rations, which we received at noon, were a thin soup, which had almost no nutritional value and was made of rotten vegetables, and about two hundred grams of bread.

Sometimes, usually on Sundays, we would get cooked potatoes, which we would eat with the skins on, or cooked noodles. Each of the barracks had a dining room with tables and chairs, and each man had a permanent seat.

One man sat at the head of the table. He was responsible for receiving and distributing the food. In order to divide it fairly, he would use the standard system. He would cut the bread into eight or ten pieces. (I do not remember the exact number.) In turn, one of the other men would get up and turn his back to the distributor, who would point with the knife to one portion and ask, "Whose?" When the answer was given, the designated man would take his portion, and the process would continue until everyone had received a share. As I wrote earlier, we used the same method in Spilve. Every crumb mattered to us, and therefore, we invented this system to ensure that no one would be deprived.

Most of the Jews, especially the older ones, were weakened by hardship and hunger, even before we got to Magdeburg. I recall two deaths, Jewish acquaintances of mine who came from the Kovno ghetto and Stutthof. They were both bloated from hunger and did not survive.

Several of my acquaintances from the Spilve labor camp in Riga were also together with me in the Polte labor camp: Micha Greenberg and Abba Tzapp, who had been the SS-appointed overseer in charge of all the Jewish men in Spilve. They both worked as painters and reported to Kagan. In addition, I knew Yaakov Briker, who had come to Spilve from the Kovno ghetto, and Sioma Sorkin from Riga, also with me in Spilve.

By chance, I met a Jew in his fifties named Nemenchinsky, who told me that when I was three years old, he had been quite friendly with my parents. He also told me many stories about his life in Kovno before the war.

I recall two incidents that exemplified the camp overseers' brutality. In fact, the first case actually concerned Kagan, the Jew from Riga.

Twice a day, we had to report for roll call. As always, Kagan was responsible for maintaining discipline. We were ordered to stand up straight in line and then ordered to remove our hats. Kagan would walk among the rows and check if everyone had obeyed these orders. Then, he would count us and report to Hoffmann or Schiller with the number of inmates.

During one of these roll calls, Kagan noticed that one of my buttons was unbuttoned, and so he punched me hard in the face. I nearly collapsed.

In the second incident, I was present when the Germans forced a son to give his father twenty-five strong lashes with a belt because of his "sin": Underneath his pillow, they had found part of a spare uniform. The son's name was Robert from Riga. I met his father in Vilna after the war, and he told me that his son had been shot by the SS shortly before liberation.

Throughout that winter, I carefully followed the news from the fronts via newspaper scraps that I happened to find. I sensed that this was to be the final winter of the war. The Russians in the East and the Allies in the West were trouncing Hitler's army in bloody battles. During the winter of 1945, the number of Allied aerial attacks over Germany increased, and they caused significant loss of life and property in the city of Magdeburg.

These attacks usually occurred at night, but there were occasional daytime bombardments as well. We were able to hear the reverberations. Luckily, neither our camp nor any of the adjacent camps were bombed.

Whenever we heard the siren during our shifts, we would descend into the well-built underground shelters, which, we were told, were constructed back in the 1930s in preparation for the war. We were relegated to separate rooms in the shelters, away from the German workers, who were deathly afraid that we would hurt them. Our moods improved on these occasions. We would even sing nostalgic Yiddish songs about our prewar pasts.

As I noted above, I had been released from working at the plant and had been kept in the infirmary for a few days of observation. We received the same food rations as the other prisoners, but the difference was that I did not burn calories while lying in bed.

When I saw the feeble, pale patients, I realized that I would die there if I did not find work on the outside. My friends who came to visit me told me that they were doing hard physical labor at a site located about twelve kilometers outside the camp. However, they were not hungry when they returned to camp each day because they were able to "organize" food for themselves.

This is how it worked: They were assigned to dig fortifications to deter the Red Army's offensive. Every once in a while, they would ask their SS guards for permission to relieve themselves behind the destroyed, bombed-out buildings. They would use this as an opportunity to quickly sneak down into the cellar where they would find good, delicious food in glass jars or other containers. They would eat the food on the spot, and those who dared would, of course, take something with them.

My friends told me that there was another labor site, which was only five kilometers away. But they recommended that I exert myself and choose the farther site, because one could not obtain food at the closer site. Therefore, I asked to be released from the infirmary and left with the group that had chosen the farther site.

During that same period, the plant where I had worked ceased operations. The recent spate of bombings over Magdeburg and the surrounding area also damaged the factory's electrical network. All of the machinery was silent, and thus, there was no reason for me to return to work anyway.

On my first day working on the fortifications outside the city, I felt strong pains in my legs from the long walk. In addition, the physical and emotional strain of digging with a shovel for twelve hours straight took its toll. Nevertheless, my mood improved. Each day, I grew significantly stronger—thanks to the good food that I managed to "organize" for myself and as a result of working in the open field, with the springtime sun's rays shining on my back.

I had a gut feeling that I would be liberated very soon. As we passed through the city's streets, we noticed that the locals were extremely apprehensive because the front was approaching Magdeburg itself. The increased tension was evident on their faces. Countless troops and heavy weapons were brought into the city, which had been largely destroyed by the American and British bombardments. As the days went by, the city was transformed into a frontier town, and the residents prepared to meet the enemy coming from the West.

Undoubtedly, the Germans would have preferred to surrender to the Anglo-Americans rather than to the Russians, but the choice was not theirs to make. One day, word spread that the Americans were located just a few dozen kilometers to the west of the city, and the residents received the following official instruction: Five sirens in a row would be the signal that the American armored forces were approaching the city.

On April 11, a bright spring day, after we finished yet another day of hard labor, building the fortifications, we heard the eagerly awaited sirens. Our panicked guards started fighting among themselves as they tried to figure out what to do with us: Should they immediately lead us back to the camp, take us to a shelter, or leave us to fend for ourselves?

An SS officer in his sixties, who outranked all the junior SS men, ordered one of them to gather us up quickly and take us back to the camp. However, the latter adamantly refused to obey the order, and in response, the frustrated officer threatened to have him court-martialed if he continued to disobey orders. Following a vocal argument and having no other choice, the officer ordered two other SS men to arrest the recalcitrant SS man. However, to our surprise, they both refused to detain him.

Finally, they somehow managed to compromise and to get us to line up. We were then ordered to walk quickly to the center of the city with the work tools we carried every day. But after walking a few hundred meters, we suddenly noticed that our guards had disappeared.

We spontaneously dropped our tools in the middle of the street. Each one of us was filled with jubilation over our liberation. Some cried emotionally. We kissed each other and enjoyed that sweet moment of freedom, without thinking about what would come next.

Instinctively, we found ourselves walking toward the camp to obtain food and a temporary shelter. We guessed that the SS men were no longer in control, and they surely had escaped from the camp.

I happened to meet up with a father and his young son from Vilna during our spontaneous exhilaration over our taste of freedom, and the three of us hurried to the camp. On the way, we saw our anxious guards, the SS men who administered the camp, scurrying in every direction with suitcases in their hands. They paid no attention to us. Clearly, we were not their main concern at that moment.

Jews from our camp greeted us. Their hands were filled with food, which they shared with us, especially the bread. Personally, after years of hunger, I "attacked" half a loaf of bread and "devoured" it within a few minutes.

Not far from the camp's gate, we came across an unexpected "scene": Drunk and pale, Paul Hoffmann and Schiller—the mass murderers' leaders—drew their pistols and ordered us back to the camp. In order to show that they were serious, they shot in the air a few times, but several moments later, they left, carrying their suitcases. Apparently, they had hoped to flee by train, bus, or any other available vehicle before fate caught up with them.

They left behind a wagon filled with food and valuables that they had amassed before escaping. We took the food and discarded the rest; we literally threw it in the street. I was just sorry that we were unable to eliminate those two monsters.

When we approached the camp's gate, which was wide open and unguarded, we realized that we were starting a new stage in our lives. We entered and saw that pandemonium reigned in the camp where we had suffered so much. After looking around, I found a civilian hat and jacket. I entered the home of some German civilians and asked them to replace my striped pants as well, but they refused to help me.

Many Jews—the camp's former inmates—managed to replace their striped uniforms and hats before scattering in every direction. Their plan was to hide out in the city until the American Army arrived.

Meanwhile, those who remained in the erstwhile camp feasted on the abundant food that they found in the warehouses they now controlled. Many were unable to control their appetites. They got sick and writhed in pain, but they did not receive medical attention.

After tasting a few delicacies, I left the camp with a number of other Jews in search of a temporary hiding place until our final liberation.

We knew that in the city, there were still many armed soldiers, including members of the *Volkssturm* and the *Fausten*. The former were armed civilians, ranging from pre-military age to men in their sixties. Distraught and on edge, they roamed the city's streets in small groups. The *Fausten*, armed with anti-tank weapons, were particularly conspicuous in the city. Most of them were young and wore military uniforms. (*Faust* is the German word for fist.)

Fortunately, they did not notice us, and we were able to advance safely toward our destination but not for long. After running to save time, while avoiding the main streets, we reached a prison courtyard. There were no guards at the entrance. Suddenly, from the multistoried prison's windows, we heard the prisoners' voices speaking in various foreign languages. Hand movements accompanied the voices, as if to say: You have already been liberated, and we send you our blessings and hope that we will be liberated too!

At that moment, we heard a German shout, "Halt!" Someone in the prison's administrative building had seen us. We went in and figured that we were trapped. However, a quick clarification by telephone, and we were released. We breathed sighs of relief!

As we continued onward, we chanced upon some Red Cross workers distributing hot soup from a large vat to anyone who asked. We requested food and received bread and hot soup. They treated us kindly. One of the locals gave me a pair of pants and a shirt, and I put them on instead of my striped uniform.

Together with many other former prisoners, I spent the night under the railway bridge, on the cold concrete. However, I was so exhausted and excited that I nevertheless fell asleep and slept until the morning.

Thursday, April 12

Early that morning, we received a hot meal from the same Red Cross workers. We wondered if that place would serve as a suitable temporary solution to our current predicament. We were treated humanely, and there were no SS men to be seen. However, our feeling of uncertainty troubled us.

We kept waiting to hear the American tanks entering Magdeburg. However, when they did not materialize, we all decided to return to the camp to get enough food for several days and then to leave and find a relatively secure hiding place. By the time we came to a decision, the springtime day had ended, and it was evening when we arrived back in the camp. Many of the camp's former inmates were gone. Those who still remained were led by several of the more energetic young people, who tried to maintain some semblance of order and discipline among the onetime prisoners.

Later that evening, some Volkssturm members arrived and ordered us to obey wartime safety regulations and to go to the nearest shelter, in the women's camp. Before entering the shelter, I prepared a package of food, mainly bread and cans of sardines, in case I would be forced to hide. In addition, I made sure that I was not hungry. Two young men from Lithuania, one from the city of Rakishok and the second from Kovno, I believe, were with me. Following a brief discussion, we decided to go to the shelter. It was pitch black and very crowded, and there was no room to sleep.

In the morning, we heard that the camp was surrounded by armed Volkssturm men. We exited the shelter, and within a few minutes, a Volkssturm man appeared and said that due to military considerations, the Polte plant where we had worked was to be blown up. We, the former workers, were to be transferred to a different camp in the East. He did not tell us the name of the camp. Under the circumstances, I had no choice but to obey these orders.

We were ordered to line up in rows of three, the men in front, and the women in the back. The Jewish women, most of them from Hungary, lined up behind us, together with the young Ukrainian women, who constituted the majority.

Under heavy guard, we left the camp and marched to the Elbe River via the center of Magdeburg. We felt helpless. We were trapped, and there was no way out. Our guards made sure that no one stepped out of line.

After searching the courtyards of the nearby houses, the guards managed to round up several young Jewish men and one Jewish woman, whom they beat severely. When we approached one of the bridges spanning the Elbe River, our guards noticed a swarthy Italian man and suspected that he was a Jew. They shoved him into the rows of Jewish men, but when they heard him speaking Italian, they released him.

After crossing the bridge and continuing eastward for several kilometers, we suddenly made an abrupt left turn onto a soccer field, where we were allowed to rest. A truck arrived with the feeble and sick Jews from the infirmary where I had stayed. They were all elderly Jews, who could barely stand on their own two feet. Some Jewish men from our camp managed to find hiding places in the city and thus avoided this additional torment. Those who arrived by truck were left in the tennis courts.

The entire field was enclosed in a three-meter-high fence. The Jewish and Ukrainian women lay down on the soccer field, and the armed guards allowed us to eat the food we had brought with us. I had bread and a can of sardines. Somehow, I managed to open the can, and after tasting the fish with great relish, I started to eat.

Meanwhile, we noticed that an airplane was flying overhead at a low altitude. We did not care whose plane it was or where it was going. Several minutes later, we heard a sharp whistle, and then an artillery shell landed in the tennis court, where we were eating and resting ahead of our march onward.

The scene was truly horrifying: blood, body parts flying through the air, the wounded crying out in pain. A man named Feur from Kovno was killed instantly. We had walked together the entire way and had spent much of the time talking. His wife and two daughters were with me in Spilve in Riga. He, too, had spent some time in that camp. He told me that miraculously, he had escaped unscathed when he and a group of Jews from the ghettos were forced to walk through a minefield to clear it for the German Army. But now his luck had finally run out.

I also saw a doctor from Riga moaning in agony. The powerful explosion had blown one of his hands away. I believe his name was Bruno May.

And then, a number of young Jews and I spontaneously began ripping up the eastern part of the fence. Then, one by one, we started to crawl through the hole.

Since the bombardment continued along our escape route through the soccer field where the women were located, there were many casualties. Everything was one big jumble: the blasts of the shells landing among these unfortunate women and the shrieks of the wounded. The entire area was covered in dense smoke. As we ran, we occasionally looked back, because we surmised that, in spite of all the confusion, our guards were not sitting idle.

When we finally escaped the field of fire and reached a nearby village, the sounds of the explosions and the victims' cries continued to reverberate in our ears. We entered an empty house. Based on the leftover food and clothing we found lying around, we figured that freed prisoners or other people who were fleeing their captors had been in the house not too long before. We found notes written in Russian, as well as about three kilograms of carrots and some canned food, which, hungry as we were, was a treasure trove for us.

We debated whether or not we should remain in the open house where anyone could come in. There were seven of us: me, the Sorkin brothers from Riga (Sioma, the older one, was in Spilve with me, and Grisha, the younger one, worked in the galvanization department in Polte), Chalfin and Michelson from Riga, Vatkin from Kovno, and Bandet from Lodz. We decided to stick together until we were liberated. As evening approached, we searched for a place to sleep until the situation cleared up. We wanted to be very sure that our pursuers, the German guards, had disappeared for good.

Across from the empty house was a small, unguarded factory. We decided to spend the night there. Rather than spread out, we all preferred to remain close together near the factory's entrance. There we found a wooden hut. The door was open. Without thinking about it too much, we went inside and found places for ourselves in the corner against the outer wall, facing the entrance. We lay down atop black flammable blocks (briquettes) used for heating houses and spent the night listening carefully for any sounds or voices coming from outside.

Saturday, April 14

When we woke up early that morning in hopes of finding a more secure hiding place, we were surprised to see one of the factory workers standing in the doorway. Noticing our startled faces, he reassured us in broken German but suggested that we leave the plant before the owner, a Gestapo man, arrived. He added that he himself was French and that the owner, an extremely cruel man, would show no mercy and would not hesitate to hand us over to the Nazi authorities, who had not yet surrendered. We thanked him, and without too much thought, we left the factory.

Fortunately, not too far away, we found barracks belonging to Russian prisoners of war, who apparently had worked and lived in the factory. In one of the barracks, which resembled the hut where we had been the day before, we found various items in the rooms as well as leftover food. All the signs indicated that when the prisoners had heard the nearby artillery fire the day before, they had fled.

After a short while, a number of Ukrainian women and several lone Jews—men and women—began arriving at the abandoned barracks. Like us, they had escaped yesterday's inferno at the soccer field. Little by little, our group came together. We divvied up the leftover food we had found in the kitchen, and we slept on the wooden beds in the bedrooms where we also found linens and blankets. The women slept in a separate but adjacent room.

After spending three days and nights in that relatively secure location, we were able to unwind a bit after everything that had happened to us. We tried to build up our strength, because we had no idea what the coming days would bring. As we were well aware, the entire area was swarming with Hitler's supporters, who refused to recognize that his downfall was imminent.

We could hear powerful echoes of the fighting, coming from the direction of Magdeburg, a clear sign that the city would soon fall into the U.S. Army's hands.

On Tuesday morning, April 17, we were surprised to see a Volkssturm man enter our barracks. It is not hard to imagine how it felt to see one of our tormenters again. Armed with an automatic weapon, he did not ask who we were or what we were doing there. Instead, he simply ordered us to go outside and start marching with him and some of his armed friends toward the town of Koenigsborn.

They told us that we were under their protection, and they would ensure that we all had food and lodging. We would be sent to work every morning.

We soon arrived in Koenigsborn where two armed Wehrmacht soldiers assumed control of us. They actually treated us well and brought us to the village of Biederitz, located three kilometers to the left of the main highway leading eastward to Berlin.

When we arrived in the village, the German soldiers divided us into work groups. Our job was to build fortifications in and around the area. No one in the village knew that we were Jewish. When they asked us about our nationality, we said that we were Ukrainians. In fact, the German soldiers suspected that we were actually Jewish because we all spoke German. However, they pretended not to notice.

Like the other former prisoners, we received viable food rations, including 400 grams of bread, margarine, and even sugar and sausage. We also collected some food from the locals, who were willing to help us. The Germans put us up in an abandoned house on the village outskirts. The living conditions were rudimentary. But since we sensed that our final liberation was approaching, we were even willing to suffer a bit if necessary and accepted the situation.

There were only six of us. The others, including Vatkin, who had escaped with us from the soccer field, left us to search for living quarters in a different area. As a result, we became a family.

The work was not too difficult for us, because we had endured hard labor. They did not pressure us either, and the spring weather improved our spirits. There were rumors in the village that the Americans were now in control of Magdeburg.

We finished the job in a week, and then a German soldier took us to the village of Menz, located about six kilometers from Biederitz and about ten kilometers from Magdeburg. Our first impression, based on the amazingly well tended homes and gardens, was that there were no indications that Germany had been involved in such a vicious war. However, the villagers' faces revealed that they were anxious and scared about what would soon happen to them.

The village leaders provided us living quarters in an abandoned school and food rations, which were equivalent to the food we had in Biederitz, the previous village.

Every day, from 8:00 a.m. until midnight, we dug defensive ditches at a site located several kilometers away. When we walked there, the same lone German soldier who had brought us to Menz escorted us. He treated us with indifference as if to say, "What's the point of all this extra work?"

A group of prisoners-of-war from Western countries lived in the same abandoned school as we did. They spoke Spanish, French, and Italian. In addition, the school housed several Ukrainian women who had managed to escape the soccer field under the German guards' fire. In spite of the cultural differences, we all managed to find a common language. In particular, the Spanish and the French frequently tried to entertain us. They sang and told jokes in German, which we, of course, all knew, and thus, they raised our morale. The Ukrainian women sang songs in Russian or Ukrainian. However, we simply could not sing. We had suffered too much during those terrible years.

As was the case in Biederitz, when we lacked a bit of bread or potatoes, we turned to the local Germans. Here, too, nearly everyone, with just a few exceptions, was willing to help us. Bandet from Lodz, a plump, short, and broad-shouldered young man in his early twenties from our group, was especially skilled at this type of "begging." He would stand at the door, a piteous expression on his face, looking as if he were about to burst into bitter tears. Immediately, the locals would bring him the food he requested. He always used the same words, "I'm hungry, ma'am. Please give me something to eat!"

One day in late April, word arrived from the front that Hitler's military commanders were fighting for their lives. The Red Army was waging fierce battles on the outskirts of Berlin, and in many places, the Allied armies had reached the Elbe River. The chief murderers, including Hitler, Himmler, Goebbels, Mussolini, and their ilk, were no longer alive. They had committed suicide, were executed in a public hanging (as was the case with Mussolini), or were captured. In short, the war was coming to an end, and mankind would soon be able to breathe a sigh of relief. The long nightmare was finally coming to an end.

In early May, Menz's local authorities stopped providing us with food. This did not really affect us, the Jews, because we had been stockpiling food from the locals in case of emergency.

In addition, it so happened that an artillery shell had killed a horse during one of the incessant bombardments. Word spread quickly among the locals, and when we saw that they were running toward the road, we followed with knives, which we somehow managed to acquire. When we arrived at the site, we saw the dead horse lying on its side in the middle of the road. A few Germans, who had arrived before us, were already "at work." They cut off pieces of meat from the carcass. We were also able to collect several kilograms of horsemeat that day. In my entire life, horsemeat had never passed my lips, but at that point we were not very picky. We decided to make a "celebration" for ourselves.

It had been ages since we had tasted soup and especially cooked meat. Thus, we obtained cooking utensils, and after finding bricks and some wood in the school's courtyard, we started to cook, each man according to his own culinary abilities. That evening, we enjoyed a meal of meat and vegetable soup made of whatever ingredients we had been saving up.

By that time, early May, we no longer saw any German soldiers in the area. And more importantly, there were no SS men around either. Apparently, some of them had been sent to the final, decisive battle for Berlin, and the others simply changed out of their uniforms and escaped as refugees from their places of residence. They tried to hide from justice, which would soon force them to pay for their crimes.

Even among the local population, there were those who played a role in the process that led to the murder of Europe's nations and especially the Jewish people. These Germans now feared for their own safety as well as that of their families. Many of them simply shut themselves up in their homes and awaited their fates.

Personally, I felt more secure and calmer by the day. I decided to look around for a medical office or a private doctor, who could treat the wounds on the back of my neck. These sores had first appeared in the winter of 1944 when I was in the Spilve labor camp. They were caused by vitamin deficiency, and during that pre-liberation period, they really started to bother me. I soon located a young German female doctor, who worked in her own private clinic. She treated me both kindly and professionally and offered to help me however she could.

My appointment was on Friday, May 4. I told her in German, which I knew well, what had happened to me as a Jew in the ghetto and the labor and concentration camps under the Nazi regime and about my family and people's fate during that horrible era. Her agonized expression showed me that she was shocked by my story. Following the initial treatment, she gave me a second appointment for Sunday, May 6, even though it came out on her day of rest.

Meanwhile, the situation continued to develop at a dizzying pace. On that Friday, after I returned to our lodgings at about noon, I noticed many white notes on the ground in front of the school. The notes, which were printed in German and English, declared unambiguously and categorically that the local inhabitants were ordered to remove, on their own, all the obstacles and fortifications they had erected by the following day. The Allied armies were arriving. We waited impatiently for the next day to see our liberators arriving in the village. Liberation had finally come!

On Saturday afternoon, May 5, we stood along the main road ahead of our liberators' arrival. And then, a number of trucks started coming from the direction of Magdeburg. In each truck, senior officers of the defeated Wehrmacht were standing, crowded together. The insignias had been removed from their uniforms, but their elegant, ironed clothes testified to their senior ranks within Hitler's army.

Many of the villagers stood next to us and watched the unusual spectacle as they wiped tears from their eyes. The trucks with their unconventional "cargo" moved eastward. They were followed by several minibuses, which stopped in front of us and asked who we were. When we said that there were many liberated prisoners from various Nazi labor camps here in the village of Menz, they immediately turned into the village. There were both officers and civilians among them.

We led them to our temporary dwellings. The senior officers asked each one of us where we were headed. Did we want to go west or did we prefer to wait to be liberated by the Red Army? After a brief consultation, the six of us Jews decided unanimously that we would not travel with them. And then, they informed us that the next day, Sunday, May 6, the Red Army's advance units were due to arrive from the East!

The rest of the people, who had announced that they wanted to go westward, boarded the minibuses. We said goodbye with hugs and kisses.

Naturally, the Ukrainian women and girls were pleased to hear that the Red Army units were on their way. They stayed with us to await the soldiers' arrival because we also intended to travel eastward. We were excited and relieved. At long last, we would be free.

CHAPTER EIGHT:

Liberation, Convalescence, and the Red Army

Sunday, May 6

Early that morning, we once again headed out to the main highway between Magdeburg and Berlin in eager anticipation of the day's events. Excited, we stood on the side of the road, looking eastward, and waited.

At last, there they were—the intelligence corps, followed by the Red Army's mechanized units! Our joy had no bounds. We welcomed them warmly, with handshakes and hugs.

From the beginning, our liberators realized that we, the Jews and the Ukrainian women, were their true friends, and that we were willing and able to help them with intelligence. After all, we spoke both languages, Russian and German.

A Russian officer invited me to join him at a restaurant, which was located near the highway. He asked me to tell the restaurant owner, in German and in the officer's name, that he should provide the best service and clean, tasty food to the customers. I realized that the officer wanted to make a point: "Look, from now on, we're in charge here!"

After that public visit, I accompanied the same officer and several intelligence troops to a number of private homes in the village. But to our surprise, all the houses were empty. The residents had left everything behind because they were afraid that an inspection of their personal papers would reveal that they had cooperated with the Nazi regime. They simply fled in great haste: Breakfast was still on the table, the beds were unmade, and the closets were wide open. Only their valuables and their personal documents were missing.

Every house that we visited was furnished in exquisite taste and elegantly appointed, and the cellars were all stocked with food, including cheese, sausage, ham, lard, and various jellies. In accordance with the German custom, everything was neatly arranged on the shelves and stored in special crocks, which kept the food fresh for extended periods. Each crock had a label, indicating the date the food was preserved as well as the expiration date. In addition, wine racks held bottles of assorted alcoholic beverages.

The Russian soldiers wanted vodka, and when they did not find any, they "took revenge" on the bottles of cognac, whiskey, and wine. They opened every bottle, took a few gulps, and then smashed the bottles on the cellar walls. The accompanying officer did not approve and reminded them, "Remember why we're here. Search for documents."

However, no documents were to be found in any of the homes until we reached the last house. There, in a remote corner of the cellar, we found an open safe, containing documents, which attested to the owner's identity and his membership in the SS, as well as valuables, such as jewelry, hundreds of German marks, and watches. The officer let me take two gold rings and a wristwatch for myself.

Before we reached the cellar, he had also allowed me to take some civilian clothing and shoes. He was kind to me, because he saw how I was dressed.

That evening, I decided to go see the German doctor, who had told me to return for a second treatment of my neck sores. She was in a depressed mood. Visibly upset, she told me that a Russian soldier had forcibly removed her wristwatch. Nevertheless, she took good care of me and did not charge me. She knew I could not pay her.

I took leave of her and returned to my friends in the school, which continued to serve as our residence. Throughout the evening and the night, we could hear sounds of joy and singing coming from the adjacent rooms. The Ukrainian women and girls were celebrating in their rooms with their liberators. Needless to say, they had plenty of alcohol.

For us, the six Jews, it was a very emotional night. We wondered about the future that awaited us. Our primary concern was how to search for our surviving relatives, because we still hoped that maybe some of our loved ones had somehow managed to stay alive.

My mind raced. I was too excited to sleep.

Monday, May 7

I spent the day working with soldiers and officers of the Red Army's intelligence corps, searching for German suspects among the villagers. In the evening, one of the officers informed us that we should prepare to leave the village of Menz the next day.

Tuesday, May 8

At around 8:00 a.m., we gathered our belongings and assembled in the designated meeting place on the village outskirts where we found several dozen German men, residents of the village. They stood in orderly lines and awaited further instructions. After a short while, the Germans and we were told to march eastward, escorted by Russian soldiers.

We walked dozens of kilometers, with short breaks for resting, eating, and drinking. As evening approached, we arrived in a town whose name I have forgotten. The soldiers took the Germans to a building in the center of town for questioning, and after a quick supper, we were led to an empty warehouse to rest. We were exhausted from the long walk and lay down on the wooden floor. I used a pile of boxes, which I had found in the warehouse, as a mattress and my bundle of clothing as a pillow.

I must have slept very soundly, because I did not even notice when someone stole the bundle right out from under my head. Apparently, one of our Russian escorts assumed that my package contained some sort of treasure and took advantage of my deep sleep. Thus, I was left with only the clothes on my back.

'It's good I didn't get undressed,' I told myself. 'Otherwise, I'd be left naked.'

Wednesday, May 9

In the morning, following a quick breakfast, several Russian soldiers told us that we had to walk with them to the next town, which was located a few kilometers away, to be interrogated in a military office.

The day before, when we had marched dozens of kilometers, I noticed that we had not seen a single person in uniform, neither German prisoners nor Red Army officers or soldiers. This seemed odd to us.

But today, just as we started walking, we saw a large group of Russian soldiers with their officers rejoicing, cheering, and even throwing their hats in the air. When we approached and asked them why they were so happy, their one-word reply spoke volumes, "Victory!" The cruel war was finally over!

The shining eyes of the tested, exhausted troops said everything. We felt that on that fateful day, a new era had begun for humanity as a whole and especially for our nation, the Jewish people, who had endured such terrible suffering during the war. Victory Day, May 9, the day Nazi Germany was defeated, is etched in my memory forever.

At that moment, I said to myself, 'Fortunate is the man whose suffering and torment drove him to the outer limit of human endurance yet managed to survive, unbroken, and to reach this joyous occasion. And I am one of those people.'

But at the same time, I thought of the millions of people—both Jews and non-Jews—who had paid with their lives and did not live to see their oppressors' downfall.

We went to the Russian military intelligence office for a short interrogation. They asked me all sorts of personal questions: Where and when was I born? What happened to me during the war? And finally, "How did you manage to stay alive?!"

I replied, "I guess that's what Fate wanted!"

When the interrogation was over, we were taken to a convalescent camp for survivors of the various concentration camps. The living conditions were very comfortable, especially for us, the victims of misery and hunger. Our group of six was split up. Each one of us was placed in a different ward. The large convalescent camp was located in a wooded area. It included a makeshift hospital, which was staffed by skilled professionals—doctors and nurses—who provided medical treatment to those in need. And there was no lack of patients. I, too, was examined, but fortunately, I did not require any medical assistance. However, they recommended a recovery period until I regained my strength.

We were given three full meals a day, and every evening, we watched popular Russian films on an outdoor movie screen. The springtime weather was very pleasant; it did not rain during that period.

After recuperating for three weeks, I felt much stronger, and I had gained a significant amount of weight.

In late May, military officials compiled a detailed list of everyone in the convalescent camp who had recovered by then. Since, according to the identity card that I had received during the prewar Soviet era, my birthday was January 8, 1922, the military officials decided to draft me.

Shalom Sorkin and I were the only ones from our group to be sent to the army. The two men from Lodz were permitted to return to their hometown. Sorkin's brother Hirsch'le, who suffered from lung disease, was sent to recover in a sanatorium in the Crimea, and Vatkin, the Jew from Kovno, was free to return to Lithuania.

Thus I became a private in one of the Fourth Brigade's battalions, which was part of the Fifth Army, led by Marshal Zhukov. The Fifth Army belonged to the Third Front under Marshal Sokolovsky's command. Among other victories, our brigade captured Berlin.

The brigade was based in the forests around Berlin, and we lived in tents. Our training lasted several weeks, and then, at the end of June, our battalion was transferred to a number of three-story buildings on the outskirts of Potsdam. The buildings were built in the shape of a square. In the center, there was a large field, which was used for drills, roll calls, performances, and so on.

Military life was not overly strenuous for me, and I adjusted rather quickly. I had regained my strength and was able to get through the weapons training, even at night, wearing a gas mask and carrying bags of sand on my back. Sometimes the commanders would reverse our schedules: Daytime operations were conducted at night. We each received 800 grams of bread and three meals a day. For me, this was a lot, and the army toughened me both physically and emotionally.

My main concern during this period was the fact that I had been unable to learn anything about my sisters' fates, although I had made numerous inquiries via various channels.

In early July, I was sworn in to the Red Army. At my request, I became a member of the Komsomol because I believed in the fundamentals of Soviet socialism.

One day, something happened that significantly altered my service in the Red Army and left a lasting—and positive—impact on my future. During the morning roll call, the battalion's commander announced that he needed someone to draw a picture of Lenin. Thanks to my drawing skills, I was the only one out of the entire battalion to volunteer.

I was asked what tools I needed, and I replied, "Good drawing paper, a pencil, an eraser, and a photograph of Lenin." After breakfast, I was given everything on my list and invited to begin working in the battalion's cultural hall (known as the Red Corner). For a photograph, they brought me a newspaper clipping from the famous daily paper, *Izvestia*, which included a picture of Lenin. I finished my drawing to great acclaim, and I was even photographed while completing the final stage of the project.

From then, I served as the Red Corner's designer and was given various graphic and decorating assignments. As part of my work, I even edited our battalion's wall newspaper, although I was not yet completely fluent in Russian. My assistants were a number of Ukrainian soldiers, whose command of the Russian language also left much to be desired.

I was kept very busy with all my Red Corner work, and I was even exempt from daily training. However, occasionally, I was required to participate in brigade-wide exercises. In addition, since I was more or less fluent in German, I sometimes served as a translator for the battalion's senior officers.

There were several other Jews in my battalion; everyone else was Ukrainian. During that period, I did not experience any anti-Semitism. In fact, quite the opposite. I even became quite friendly with two Ukrainians.

Eventually, as part of my activities in the cultural hall, I organized a group of soldiers who knew how to sing. An officer served as the conductor, and I found several soldiers who could play the mandolin or the guitar. I played the mandolin, and we became a real band. We rehearsed and soon started performing for the troops and officers in our brigade's battalions. They were spread out over a wide area around Berlin, and thus, we were required to travel from place to place. I bought the musical instruments in Potsdam, using money from my battalion's commander.

Thus, time passed quickly by.

One day, I met a Jewish soldier from Dvinsk. His name was Avraham Kanolik, and he was born in 1916. We became fast friends, and he told me that he had married a girl from his city before the war. They had managed to escape to Russia together with her father and brother. Avraham was immediately drafted into the Red Army, and he had spent the war participating in many fierce battles before he and his unit arrived in Berlin. By profession, he was a tailor, and he worked in the battalion's workshop, together with several shoemakers, to meet the needs of the battalion's senior officers.

When he told me that he had been writing to his wife in Dvinsk, I asked him to inquire about my dear friend Shayna'le. The answer came back in the affirmative. She had indeed been liberated near Stutthof by the Red Army, but she was very sick and feeble and was hospitalized in Riga. I got her address, and when she recovered and left the hospital, we started to exchange letters.

In my free time, I recorded my memories in Yiddish. I wrote about everything that had happened to me during the war. The memories were still fresh and painful.

At the end of the summer, after completing a major operation, our brigade relocated. We were ordered to march, together with the brigade's mechanized and support units, some three hundred and fifty kilometers from the Berlin area to the city of Rostock on the Baltic coast.

The operation's objective was to clear the forests around Potsdam of potential enemies, ahead of the trilateral conference— the first such conference since the war ended—between Stalin, Truman, and Churchill. Our entire brigade was involved in the mission. We combed house after house, village after village. Meticulously, we searched for weapons and suspects. However, our orders explicitly stated that we were not allowed to touch the

German citizens' property, and we could detain people only when there was sufficient cause.

Toward the end of the operation, I witnessed an unusual event. I went with an officer and another soldier to the house of an elderly German couple, and during our inspection, we found a shotgun and a case of ammunition. Apparently, the husband suffered from heart disease, and out of fear and excitement, he dropped dead.

In general, the operation was a success, and there were no mishaps. And when the historic meeting was over, our brigade moved to Rostock.

We walked about thirty-five kilometers each day, with several stops to eat and drink along the way, and slept in the forests at night. Early in the morning of the tenth day, we arrived in Rostock. By that point, we were drained and exhausted, but when the brigade's orchestra started playing, we felt better.

Our battalion was based in three-story buildings in the center of town. I continued my social activities for the battalion and was able to see my good friend Avraham at his workplace nearly every day. I also found time to write in my journal in Yiddish and continued to correspond with my dear friend Shayna'le.

In September 1945, I decided to send a postcard via military post to my birthplace, Utian. I used the street and number of the house where we had lived before the war and added a note, PLEASE GIVE THIS POSTCARD TO THE FIRST JEW WHO ENTERS THE CITY'S POST OFFICE. To my surprise and great joy, within two weeks, I received a letter from my sisters, who just that month had returned to Lithuania from Serov, Russia, a city in the Ural Mountains. Their letter arrived from Vilna. By chance, one of my friends had come to Utian to search for his family, and he was given my postcard. He discovered that my sisters were living in Vilna, and he immediately forwarded my postcard to them.

That day, my mood improved dramatically. Now, at last, I had a specific place that I wanted to be after being released from the army. Immediately, I ran over to tell Avraham about the letter, and we celebrated together.

In their first letter, my sisters wrote briefly about their lives during the war. They told me how happy they were that I was alive, and soon, they believed, we would be reunited. My sisters added that they now lived at 17 Museum Street in Vilna, and they each had a steady job. Robbers had broken into their previous apartment, and now they were in desperate financial straits. They did not even have clothes to wear.

Avraham offered to help me send a package of clothing and leather soles to my sisters, and I was extremely moved by his generous gesture. I sent packages to them several times.

On February 10, 1946, I completed my journal.

In April of that year, my friend Avraham was released from his military service and returned to Dvinsk, his hometown. I gave him my journal and told him that when I was released, I would pick it up from him on my way to Vilna.

After he left, I became somewhat despondent. I no longer had anyone to visit, and I missed our heart-to-heart talks.

That same month, Shayna'le and I stopped writing to each other. In her last letter, she informed me that she had recently met a young man from Rakishok, Lithuania. She was fond of him, and they were going to get married and move to Poland. Her news did not improve my mood. I had hoped that someday we would be able to rebuild our lives together, and now my dream had come to an end.

When I wrote to my sisters about my shattered hopes, they consoled me and said that once I was released from the army, I would surely find my soul mate in Vilna.

Meanwhile, I acquired two new Jewish friends from Poland. They were both about my age, and we would occasionally get together. All three of us eagerly looked forward to the day that we would be released from the army.

I took advantage of my friendship with several Germans, who, in exchange for cigarettes I received from the army, helped me obtain various essential items of clothing for myself and for my sisters.

I had a local carpenter build a large wooden suitcase for me, and it had enough room to hold whatever I managed to get my hands on. I left the suitcase and its contents in the care of a poor German widow. Obviously, I paid her for her help.

One time, I was the sole escort of a group of Russian officers, who had been granted home leave. I accompanied them to the Berlin train station, and this assignment nearly cost me my life.

It was a rainy day in September 1946. Since the battalion's commanders knew that I was fluent in German, they decided that I would make an ideal escort and translator, armed with a rifle. Early that morning, the group of officers and I left for Berlin. We traveled in a large truck, and all the officers and the driver were armed with pistols.

In the evening, as we approached Berlin, we stopped at a restaurant in a village along the main highway. One of the officers told me to tell the owners, an elderly couple, that we wanted them to serve us food and drink, including vodka, at no cost. For myself, I ordered only black bread and a cup of milk.

After eating the requested food and drinking the vodka, the officers lay down on the floor and went to sleep. They did not allow the driver to drink any vodka, and after eating his meal, he too lay down and went to sleep. I enjoyed the food that I had ordered, and I sat down on a chair in the middle of the restaurant.

I tried hard to stay awake and alert and to maintain eye contact with the restaurant's owner. Outside, heavy rains continued to fall throughout the evening, but inside, it was warm and pleasant. The silence was broken only by the officers' and driver's loud snores.

After sitting vigilantly and attentively for several hours, I suddenly heard footsteps approaching from the counter. The owner's wife came over to me, and in a quiet, polite voice, she asked me approximately how much longer we intended to remain in their restaurant. They wanted to lock up and go home. I replied briefly that I did not know. I would ask the officers and the driver when they woke up.

I was in the middle of answering her, when one of the officers, Captain Seldekov, whose face was red from drinking vodka, suddenly jumped up. He grabbed me by my lapels and dragged me outside into the pouring rain.

"What were you talking about with that German woman?" he screamed at me. "You want to betray us with those cursed Germans! I'm going to kill you right now like a dog!"

He pointed his pistol at my head.

His shouts woke the other officers. One of them ran outside, seized the drunken officer's pistol, and pulled him back inside, saying angrily, "Seldekov, you've lost your mind! Get back inside and go back to sleep! Why are you making a whole production?" And thus, my life was spared.

A month before my military service ended, I asked one of the senior officers to grant me leave to go visit my sisters in Vilna. I had done all sorts of favors for this officer such as obtaining medicine for him on the black market for his venereal disease. He promised to respond positively to my request in the very near future. Elated, I gave him a gold ring as an advance payment for his help.

However, several days later, that same officer informed me that he was returning to Russia with his wife and apologized that he had not helped me get what I wanted. But he did not return the ring I had given him. I was extremely disappointed, because I thought that it would be a long time before I would see my sisters.

To ease his conscience, the departing officer made the gesture of sending me to the nearby town of Rostock, as part of my military duties, to take driving lessons. I lived in a military building, together with the other students, and we studied driving theory.

Classes were held daily, from morning until afternoon. I hoped to complete the course before being released from the army, but after a month of classes, I received word that my demobilization process would begin on October 22, 1946, and would last until the end of November.

During my stint in Rostock, I met a nice local German couple, and I visited them nearly every day. According to the husband, he had been incarcerated in concentration camps for many years because of his opposition to the Nazi regime. Due to his political opinions, he had been branded a communist.

Since I spoke German, he was interested in my life story, and when he heard what I had endured during the war, he was stunned. Before his arrest, that man, whose name I have forgotten, was considered a talented author and poet, a gifted artist (I saw some of his oil drawings), a successful pugilist but mainly, a warm and honest man.

At the couple's request, I got the wife a job peeling potatoes in our military kitchen. They told me that they needed extra income due to their desperate financial circumstances. But unfortunately, I was embarrassed to learn that she worked for only one day before quitting. The person in charge of the kitchen had propositioned her and asked her to sleep with him. She, of course, refused and left. This disturbing incident demonstrated that every nation and society has its own scoundrels.

Nevertheless, the German couple knew that I wanted only to help them and that what happened was not my fault. When I was released from the army, I went to say goodbye to them. They gave me an elegant picture album, and inside, the husband inscribed a beautiful dedication and a poem, which he had written in honor of the Jewish people. We bid each other a fond farewell.

Years later, I learned that the husband had been elected chairman of the writers' union in East Germany.

I started to prepare to leave the army and purchased a few other essential items for myself and for my sisters. On November 25, I boarded a train that was packed with soldiers, and we traveled via Poland to Lithuania.

After crossing the Oder River on our way from Frankfurt to Poland, we arrived at the former Prussian border where we had to get off the train for a security inspection. We then continued on into Prussia.

At the Innsbruck train station, we stopped and got out for a breath of fresh air. Suddenly, elderly people and children dressed in rags beset us on all sides. They begged for food. "Uncles, a piece of bread!" I realized that even after the military victory, the Russian economy was in shambles.

On November 27, 1946, I finally arrived in the Vilna train station. I rode to my sisters' house in a horse-drawn carriage, which was a typical means of transportation in those days. My brother-in-law Hillel Mezinter, who had married my older sister Chaya in May of that year, came out to meet me. He also paid the carriage driver because I had arrived without a kopeck to my name.

My reunion with my sisters was very emotional. I was able to tell them in person everything that had happened to me and to our mother Liba Raizel—may Hashem avenge her blood—since we were separated on Tuesday, June 24, 1941, and the tragic circumstances of her death. The next day, I met our relatives, the Eisen and Sharfshtein families, who had also been living in Vilna since returning from Russia. In addition, I met various friends and acquaintances from Utian.

On the third day after I arrived in Vilna, I took an early morning train to Dvinsk to meet my friend Avraham and his family and to retrieve my journal from him. They welcomed me like an old and dear friend. While in Dvinsk, I also met several Jews whom I had known from the ghetto and the fortress.

On January 3, 1947, I started working as a painter. I lived at my sister Chaya's home, and Sarah lived there too. We had a very difficult time making ends meet during that period.

In March, Chaya gave birth to a son, but three days later, she was told that he had died. We all took the news very hard. The circumstances of the baby's death made us wonder if the baby had actually been completely healthy at birth. At that time, there were rumors in Vilna that the Lithuanians were killing Jewish newborn babies. To this day, we still do not know if these rumors had any basis in truth.

My sisters' postwar lives—until they arrived in Israel (Chaya in 1966, and Sarah in 1971)—were marked by ups and downs, but overall, they were able to rebuild their lives. Chaya had a daughter and a son, and Sarah had two daughters by her husband, Shmuel Weinstein from the town of Alitus, Lithuania.

In 1948 I married Luba Teitel from the town of Vilon, Lithuania. We had three beautiful daughters—Mira, Rosa (named after my mother Liba Raizel), and Devorah. After our eldest daughter Mira married Fima Kremer of Vilna in March 1971, we made aliyah (moved to Israel) in July of that year. My dream had finally come true!

During the twenty years after our aliyah, our other two daughters got married, and we had seven grandchildren.

Sadly, after forty-four happy and successful years of marriage, my wife Luba passed away.

Today, as I write these lines, I have eight grandchildren (six granddaughters and two grandsons) and a great-grandson, who is now sixteen months old), who are a source of considerable joy for me and bestow meaning on my life.

EPILOGUE

In Israel, I met my relatives. I had corresponded with many of them from Lithuania. They welcomed us warmly, especially my mother's two sisters—Aunt Fruma, her husband Avraham, and their four children from Kibbutz Bror Chayil, and Aunt Rivka, her husband Zussman, and their two daughters and son from Tel Aviv.

In addition, I found three cousins from my father's side: Yedidya, Regina, and their two daughters from Haifa; Yitzchak, Naomi, and their children from Moshav Ben Ami near Nahariya; and Cheyna Lifshin, her husband, and their son and daughter from Tel Aviv.

I am still in touch with all of them, and we get together on both happy and sad occasions, like any large family. Some of them are no longer among the living. May their memories be blessed.

Eventually, some of my other relatives arrived from Lithuania. I am very close with my cousin Hershele Sharfshtein and his family. The two of us recently celebrated our ninetieth birthdays, and we look forward to many more years of health and happiness.

Throughout my life, I searched for—and found—other Holocaust survivors who had been with me in Dvinsk, Riga, and other places during the war.

For instance, during the 1960s, I started to write to Shayke Eivensky, who lived in the United States. Through him, I learned that my cousin, Motke Kuretsky, was also living in the United States, as were Motke's brother and his wife, who had been in the Vilna ghetto, and Shmuel Peletz from Yanova, who hid with me in the Dvinsk prison. In 1945, the Americans liberated them all from the concentration camps. Like many others, including me, they were offered the chance to immigrate to the United States, and that was what they chose to do. They put down roots and lived out their lives in the United States.

In Israel, I discovered other people whom I had met over the years such as Berkah Kaplan. We kept up our friendship throughout the years, until his death in 2010. In addition, I met Yaakov Sreisky, who lives in Givatayim, and another group from Dvinsk, who now live in Kibbutz Kfar Blum.

To my great surprise, I also met my dear friend, Shayna'le Ichilov, from Dvinsk in Israel. She had moved to Israel from Australia with her husband and children in the 1970s. I introduced her to my wife, and we got together with them a number of times over the years. She was happy and vivacious, and in 1996, she published her memoirs. Wise and funny, the book was very well received. She passed away in 1998.

From Israel, I reconnected with my mother's sisters and brother, my American aunts and uncles: Chaim, Efraim, Yocheved, Devorah, Sidney, Moshe, and Binyamin. Some of them visited us in Israel. My wife Luba and I welcomed them warmly to our home.

In 1996 during a visit to the United States, I stayed with Arlene, my Aunt Devorah's daughter. She took me to see her parents, who then lived in Cape Cod with their younger daughter Lois and her husband. They welcomed me warmly, and I had a wonderful time with them.

I met Devorah's son Richard when he visited Israel, and we developed a very special bond.

Both Devorah and her husband died over the past year. They enjoyed a long and happy life together.

Recently Richard contacted me and suggested that I have my book translated into English so that they and future generations will be able to learn more about their family and will get to read a first-hand account of their relatives' experiences during the Holocaust. He also offered to cover the expense of translating and publishing the book in English.

During that same visit to the United States, I met Shayke and Motke. Shayke wrote a book about the Holocaust, which was published in America and translated into Hebrew.

Thanks to Joseph Rochko, a historian and Holocaust scholar from Dvinsk, my book was translated and released in Russian. During the course of my conversations with Joseph, I discovered that I had met his father in the Dvinsk ghetto. In 1941 we had worked together outside the ghetto for a while, and after liberation, I met him again during my trip to Dvinsk.

In 1992 my wife Luba died of cancer, at age sixty-nine. We were married for forty-four wonderful and happy years during which we raised and taught our three daughters and gave them a warm and loving home. At that time, we had seven grandchildren. Daniel, the oldest, had already started his military service. Luba was so proud of him! Each of our grandchildren was a source of joy and pride for her. She never stopped helping the girls raise them.

In 1993 our youngest daughter, Dorit (as she is known in Israel), gave birth to another girl, Liat. As I write these lines, Liat recently started her military service. All of our older grandsons and granddaughters completed their academic studies in different subjects, and they have all found their own unique paths. One of my great-grandsons, Attay, celebrated his bar mitzvah this year, and I have two other great-grandsons: Goni, 5, and Niv, 3. My grandchildren and great-grandchildren bring me much pleasure and imbue my life with meaning.

My wife Chaya and I share a life of love and partnership, and we are still very active. I draw, write poems, play the mandolin, and translate German and Russian songs into Yiddish, and we are both part of the same choir, where Chaya has been singing for over forty years. We go to the theater, concerts, and museums and get together with our friends. During the summer months, we travel around the country and—until fairly recently—the world.

We often spend time with our family. We celebrate birthdays and the Jewish festivals, and we face each new day with contentment and happiness.

CPSIA information can be obtained at www.ICGtesting.com
Printed in the USA
BVOW07s0956130913

331117BV00001B/4/P